The Ward Melville Diary

The Ward Melville Diary

2005-2006

Joe Cuozzo

To order additional copies of this book, contact:
Xlibris Corporation
1-888-795-4274
www.Xlibris.com
Orders@Xlibris.com
62998

Contents

Preface

Lacrosse is the fastest-growing sport in America. High schools and colleges are adding programs outside the hotbeds of Long Island, upstate New York, New England, and Maryland. Thousands of additional players seek instruction, advice and insight into the game. This diary aims to fill a portion of that desire with an inside look at two seasons at a successful public high school program—my last year as sole head coach at Ward Melville, and the following year as co-head coach. During my 38 year tenure the Patriots won: 31 League Championships, 22 Suffolk County Championships, 15 Long Island Championships, 9 Downstate Championships, and 7 New York State Championships. The program made 27 appearances in the Suffolk finals, and produced 52 All-Americans, including professionals Liam Banks, Greg Cattrano and Chris Passavia of Major League Lacrosse. A woman once told me she was walking in China wearing our team sweatshirt when a man stopped her and said, "Ward Melville Lacrosse—Mankind played there." He meant Mick Foley, our high school's contribution to professional wrestling and the New York Times best-seller lists. In this diary coaches can observe a system that worked and will encounter a way to think about the game that has proven successful. Parents will find advice on the job of building a competitive lacrosse player.

Coach Joe Cuozzo

Member of the National Lacrosse Hall of Fame, the National High School Coaches Hall of Fame, the LI Metropolitan Hall of Fame, Cortland State Hall of Fame, the Suffolk County Hall of Fame. Cuozzo coached the North Team to victory in the first ever Under Armour All-American game in 2006. He is the only high school lacrosse coach to win a state championship at two different schools.

Foreword

My first memory of Joe Cuozzo dates back to 1977. I know I saw Charlie Brown tend goal for the Patriots as far back as 1973, but I can't conjure up an image of the coach. Maybe because "Charlie Brown" was a more kid-friendly name than Cuozzo. As the son of the Ward Melville Athletic Director, I'd seen a lot of high school sports by the time an image from 1977 took shape. Football, basketball, baseball, even a cross-country meet or two—the event where I first decided perspiring athletes could smell bad. But if you went to Ward Melville, as I did with the Class of 1983, and your dad was the AD, there was no sport like lacrosse and no coach like Joe Cuozzo.

It was the final seconds of the Long Island Championship game at Hofstra University, and the Patriots were down a goal. Midfielder Rich Wilkins, with just seconds on the clock, wound up and fired a missile that missed by inches. As the white ball sailed into the night, the Patriots began dropping like flies, grown men, or so they seemed to a ten-year old, falling to their knees in anguish. As the vanquished Patriots got on the school bus to go home, my dad approached Joe Cuozzo. "Tough loss," said my dad.

Cuozzo was cool and collected. "The kids did their best," he said.

I'll never forget how calm he was after such a big game.

Over the next several years coach Cuozzo would create several more memories for me, none of them described by the words "cool," "calm," or "collected." His coaching style was passionate. His demands were clear and concise. Not ambiguity or need for interpretation when Joe Cuozzo spoke. He demanded the best from his players and often got it.

And the titles kept coming: League, County, Island, State. But passion rarely comes without controversy, and legendary success does not come without pressure. Every year without fail I'd hear the grumbling. "Cuozzo won't be around much longer." That started back in 1980. Twenty-nine years ago. Still, the titles kept coming, the wins adding up.

As a player, I peaked somewhere between ninth and tenth grade. But I loved the summer camp that Cuozzo ran on the east end of Long Island, and I can still vividly recall biking to summer league practice at Murphy Junior High, that big goalie stick in my STX-gloved hand for six miles of hills with no brakes. One year I won "Best Camper," a sure sign my lacrosse future was limited.

A bunch of my buddies did well—All-American honors, full rides to Division I powerhouses. I'm best remembered for throwing first-class tantrums after giving up goals, and an unfortunate incident where Steve Diaz hit "my guys" with a shot on a day I forgot to strap on the doctor-recommended protection.

Every now and then I'd come home from around the world to visit Ward Melville, maybe take in a county championship game with my buddy Bob Betcher. With each visit I'd notice the grumbling was louder. Not from my buddies, because love him or hate him, most Ward Melville lacrosse alumni had great respect for the man and his methods. Rather the grumbling came from the community, where 22 county championships, 15 LI titles, and seven state championships were somehow not enough. Much of the grumbling came from people I knew had never picked up a stick, who said Cuozzo was just lucky. The secret was out. The winningest coach of all time didn't actually know how to coach. He'd been blessed with great players. Every year without fail. For thirty-something years.

The Ward Melville Diary covers a time when the grumbling was loudest. It's an in-depth look at the last two tumultuous years in coach's Ward Melville career. To be sure, it captures the controversy. But for me it did more. For me this fine book brought back so many memories, some better than others. Memories of so many victories and the occasional defeat. Of the panting and puffing during our West Point drills. Of friendships and rivalries, and the smell of fresh-cut grass mingled with sweat on early Saturday mornings.

Most of all it made me remember what it meant to be part of a legacy known throughout the lacrosse world—Joe Cuozzo's legacy.

Mick Foley

Head of The Harbor, New York

Author of three memoirs: Have a Nice Day, Foley is Good, and The Hardcore Diaries; two novels: Teitam Brown, and Scooter; and three children's books.

Prologue

May 31, 2004

We could have won, I was thinking on that bus ride home. We could have beaten the eventual Long Island champion West Islip in our semifinal at Rocky Point. We hit two pipes and bungled three fast breaks, got a few bad calls, and lost 7-4. I'm proud of the 2004 Ward Melville Patriots. We were young, a junior-powered line-up. We made the mistakes of youth and paid the price. Unfortunately, we can't win it all every year, though some people think we should.

I turned around in my seat and faced a disappointed group of teenage boys. I told them I was proud of their efforts, but that it was time to continue the team tradition of the passing down the dirty socks, the treasured numbers. We'll lose a few good seniors from this team, but we retain our core group, with an undefeated junior varsity moving up. As they say, tradition never graduates.

We've got good players coming back, bright kids maturing. So does West Islip and East Islip. So does Northport. Smithtown. William Floyd. Both Sachems. Half Hollow Hills and Middle Country. Winning the Class A championship in Suffolk County gets tougher every year as youth lacrosse blossoms, everybody with feeder programs like our own Three Village Lacrosse. The road to New York State Championships usually runs through West Genesee, an upstate New York program that has mirrored our own good fortune and plays a team game that is hard to disrupt and harder to duplicate. The enemy coaching gets better and more creative, with summer camps and position clinics and personal trainers. I am getting older. More reflective and less impulsive, I hope. It's been five years since we won back-to-back New York State titles with the best high school team I ever saw. I sometimes hear I've lost my mojo, my best days are behind me . . . I should hand the job to former assistants and play golf.

Well, golf is fine, but I still love lacrosse, and the boys who play it, not just at Ward Melville, but everywhere. I still learn something every day, and I still know how to spot the thoroughbreds. And, as I have often felt, the team Ward Melville can field next year could be special. Leaders must step forward, youngsters grow up on the job. The boys will need to discipline themselves, and resist the temptations of youth as we play one of the toughest schedules in the country. And I will need to be at the top of my game.

Our community expects no less.

#

Lacrosse was invented by Native Americans, and used for conflict resolution and warrior training. The fields were huge and the game could last for days. A thousand men played on a field that stretched for miles. Players were injured and killed. In the nineteenth century the game became less violent and more of a sport. The field was shortened and players limited to ten a side: three attackmen, three midfielders, three defensemen and a goalie. Clubs were formed. Rules devised. They play the game indoors on hockey rinks in Canada, but in America we play it on football fields. It resembles soccer with sticks, hockey in the air. It has been called the fastest game on two feet and there is a place on the field for athletes of any size. Some of my best players over the years have been small guys with big hearts. Tim and Dennis Goldstein were both NCAA Players of the Year and were slender and of average height. You'll meet them and others as I document the present and reflect on the past. We have done some incredible things here at Ward Melville. And every year we have to do it all again.

2005 Pre-Season

March 8

We're having trouble getting started. Junior defenseman Sam DeVore is limping from a leg injury left over from basketball. Sam is sandy-haired and broad-shouldered, the son of a lawyer in the District Attorney's office who played his college lacrosse at UMass. Sam's running mate Andrew Maurer (Towson) is one of our toughest kids, on the varsity since ninth grade, but now he's got a chronically sore shoulder I worry about. They are members of last year's LI Empire State Games team and we'll build around them. Other attacks will hate to play us.

The weather hasn't helped my mood. I've been stuck in eastbound traffic on Rt. 347 in a blizzard for two hours, and I am stewing about our snow-covered playing field, and two scrimmages next week against tough teams that would love to knock off Ward Melville. They, of course, have artificial turf and are working outside every day. We play on grass and mud, fields that have . . . a winning tradition, a thirty-eight year won-lost record of 665-68, almost ten victories for every defeat.

I'm grumpy because it's tryouts, the worst part of the season. I know how bad these boys want to make the team, to wear that green-and-gold Patriots jacket around town. I know how hard these kids have tried to step into the shoes of players before them. Heck, people move here so their kids can play here. And it's not cheap. The Three Village school district on the North Shore of Suffolk County covers some gorgeous real estate, with waterfront homes, cozy harbors and private beaches. Old Field has two-acre zoning and is considered the eastern end of F. Scott Fitzgerald's Gold Coast. The main campus of Stony Brook University lies within the district, with 22,000 students and 15,000 employees and a teaching hospital. Neighborhoods in the southern end of the school district, the more moderately priced areas,

15

would be the nicest sections of many other Long Island districts. People pay big taxes to live here. They demand results. Our science programs produce Intel winners. Girls swimming has won 15 Suffolk County titles in a row. Our fencers never lose and we place ten percent of our senior class in the Ivy League, athletes or not. There are some parents who argue that we should keep every boy who wants to play on our team, and play every boy on our team in every game. To them I say, "Then my players get automatic As in all their subjects."

No deal? Fine. Then, let's agree varsity sports are also competitive.

And we do stress their schoolwork. If they want to advance to college, they need good grades. This is not football or basketball, and there are not so many Division I programs. A famous football coach once said he could get bacteria admitted to his university. It is not that way in lacrosse.

At this time of year it falls on me to break some wonderful hearts, but there are only so many minutes of playing time, so many jerseys. In our elementary schools we have a hundred boys per class on the lacrosse field. The fifteen per class who make our varsity have survived a dog-eat-dog marathon. This in no small measure accounts for our success, boys pushing each other to improve. They go to summer camps, together and separately, and play in the Three Village summer league, with games at Stony Brook University's LaValle Stadium, one of the best facilities in the country. We play in a fall-ball league at Farmingdale State. We do speed training. We hold captains' practices in the gym on winter Sundays. Nobody picks up the stick on the first day of tryouts and makes this team. You live with your stick. Not your skateboard. Not your video games. Not your girlfriend. Your lacrosse stick. Show me the kid who walks around town cradling a ball and I show you my future all-county attackman.

At tryouts we watch the guys do groundball drills, checking their athleticism and their skills. We preach fundamentals, keeping the back hand low, bending over and accelerating through the ball, coming up and cradling to open space. We test their passing and catching skills, standing still and on the run, weaving, over-the-shoulder passes and catches, to see how comfortable they are with their right and left hands. Everybody uses both hands, even the long-poles. The goal is to play the game the way the Indians play it, whipping the ball from ear-hole to ear-hole, never a muff.

In selecting our defenders, we look for foot-speed, agility, toughness and brains. Size is nice, and we have plenty this year, but we start with footwork, good positioning and an understanding of the game. And swagger, but not cocky or obnoxious. There is a difference.

Our middies are our thoroughbreds. They play defense with short-sticks, handle the ball in transition, and play some offense; though at Ward Melville, we usually run our offense through our attack. With those all-important attackmen, we look at stick protection, passing and shooting skills. Accuracy. And foot-speed. We want creative attackmen. Sneaky people. Speedy, sneaky people. We work on recognizing when we "have numbers", and how to take advantage.

Our goalies must have great hand-eye coordination, great reflexes, leadership skills, courage, and a short memory. No moping after goals. No head hanging. Take the ball out of the net and give it to the official. There isn't a person watching that wants to trade places with you. Get ready for the next one.

#

I was a football player at Cortland State in upstate New York, and ran track for two years in the off-season. But my roommate was a lacrosse player, and he convinced me to try out. I made the varsity and played my last two years, then eight more as a member of the Suffolk Lacrosse Club. I got my first teaching job in the Bay Shore school district, doing elementary physical education, then I taught five years of middle-school science. But there was no boys' lacrosse at Bay Shore and no desire for any. I moonlighted as a high school referee. The last game I worked was the LI Championship game in 1966 between Huntington and Manhasset. My partner was the great Al Blau.

That year a new school district on the north shore of Suffolk was looking for a lacrosse coach, and I was itching to spend more time with the game I love. I didn't worry about a cut in pay or losing seniority or sick days. I sent my name to Ward Melville and they hired me. Most of the years I taught and coached at Ward Melville, I lived with my wife and children in the Connetquot school district, a nice neighborhood, mind you, but not as snazzy as Old Field or Stony Brook or Poquott. My son Kris made All-Long Island in football, and played long-stick midfielder for the University of Massachusetts. My daughter Kim was a teacher in the Three Village school district.

Ward Melville, the man, was a shoe tycoon. His family owned estates in Old Field and Stony Brook, and they had the foresight to preserve for the public swaths of woodlands they donated for use as public schools, including the acres that became Stony Brook University. Not so many people remember the shoe stores, but Ward's name has been synonymous with a great public high school and excellent lacrosse. I feel like he got his money's worth.

#

In these days of balanced shafts, quality mesh and plastic heads, people forget what the old days were like. What I remember most of my early days were the endless hours I spent repairing wooden sticks, using fiberglass and screws on broken poles, tongue depressors to firm up catgut sidewalls, fixing throat stops. I would spend hours on Saturdays at Wolfs' Sporting Goods in Rockville Center to find the perfect long-poles, at least until 1970, when rubber heads appeared and stick repair became simpler. The early helmets were leather, and the goalies wore football pants or baggy sweats. The ball was on the ground more, and there was more head-to-head hitting. Still, if your team could pass and catch, you could stay in the game with anybody. We won a lot of games when we did not have the better athletes.

#

Ward Melville always has a bunch of guys playing big-time ball in college. This year we have Mike Ward at Duke, Nick Gentilesco at Brown, Ryan Preuss at Towson, Will Konczynin at Stony Brook, Tom Theodorakis at Syracuse, Nick Miaritis at Georgetown, Ian Applegate, the Funt brothers and Chris Mele at Wesleyan, Billy Granger at Tufts, and so many others. Greg Cattrano, Chris Passavia, Liam Banks and Drew Casino are currently pros in the MLL. Todd Sauerbrun is still a punter in the NFL.

Here's a little story about professional goalie Greg Cattrano that will show what kind of district this is. On Halloween a few years back, one of our youngsters, a peewee goalie, wanted to trick-or-treat as Greg Cattrano. His mother found a website that offered custom-made costumes. She arranged delivery and the day before Halloween the uniform arrived. It was cheesy, she said, and the name on the jersey was misspelled. One T. The little boy refused to wear it and ran up to his room, distraught. Mom called Rich Pruess, who has given years to Three Village lacrosse. Did he know of someplace she could get a better jersey? Rich said he'd see what he could do. A couple of hours later the real Greg Cattrano knocks on the boys' door. He loans the kid his real Bayhawks jersey to wear trick-or-treating that night, and throws in a pair of Brown University lacrosse shorts the boy can keep. Suddenly our young goalie is the happiest kid in Setauket. Greg never said a word to anybody and neither did Rich Preuss. They'll be mad I told the story now. But it's that kind of school district.

#

Many of the boys who get cut here could play at other high schools. Some return to the game as college students and prosper. We are three-deep in talent this year. Heck, I have seven good goalies trying out. Some schools have to beg a kid to step between the pipes. I have two Empire defenseman returning, the aforementioned DeVore and Maurer. The rising junior class is smart and athletic, and they have forced the seniors to actually lift the weights and do the running, not just brag about it. I've always found kids pushing each other to improve works best. I don't have to yell so much. Terror of losing playing-time motivates them. It's a long cold spring standing on the sideline in shorts.

My theory of preparation has always been founded on the notion that every school on Long Island has five or six good players. So those guys cancel each other out. The next fifteen guys decide the outcome of most games. At Ward Melville, our goal has always been to make our 6-thru-20 guys better than anyone else's, by a lot. We scout our opponents and plan for each game. We study our own film to improve. We look for match-ups that favor us and avoid those that don't. When things are going well, we take good shots. We take shots with a back-up in position. We stick together when things get tough. We expect to win. We practice long and hard.

#

I personally hate the cold weather, snow dripping down the back of my neck, and I think the guys listen better inside the gym on the brutal days. I know some coaches go the other way, thinking lousy conditions toughen their teams. Me, I'd rather be warm.

While we are stuck inside we work on strength and conditioning, lots of push-ups and sit-ups and jumping jacks and stretching. We do our passing and dodging drills, hoping to make these skills second nature. We "look" the ball all the way into the stick. We practice one-on-ones. Five-on-fives. Five-on-fours. Two-on-ones. I'm looking for foot-speed and stick skills, toughness, endurance, creativity, a willingness to battle.

Above us there are championship banners on the gymnasium wall, and I feel pride in what we've done here. But if I look closely, I can see that nothing spectacular has gone up since 2000, and the clock is always ticking. An opportunity lost is a chance gone forever. I can't wait to get outside and get to work. I feel us falling behind the better teams.

March 11

We get our first good action outside on the turf at LaValle. A low fog hangs over the stadium and only half the overhead lights are on. But I gotta say, we look okay. The defense is way ahead of the offense, but that's normal this early. Senior Kenny Mazzone (Siena) played well at midfield. Mazzone has been on varsity since he was freshman, and will no doubt be a captain. He is the oldest of five siblings and his Dad played at Penn. Senior Jason Ben-Eliyahu (Wesleyan) played well on the attack. His older brother Josh was a star for us. Junior long-stick midfielder Jake Westermann will see playing time this year along with junior defensemen Matt Kresse, also junior middie Kevin Kelaher. Westermann is tall and smart. His 750 Ward Melville classmates will vote him Friendliest in the Yearbook competition. Kresse is tall, thick and tough, an All-County fullback. Kelaher is muscular and quick, and his classmates vote him Most Likely to Be Famous. Sam DeVore, voted the Best Athlete of his class, is a given, one of the top defensive prospects in the nation and a superior student on the A-list for Division I colleges and the Ivies.

The rest of our starters will be seniors, boys I trust in tough spots. Maurer, Nick Ward (Maryland), Alex Blechman (Hobart), Jared Blechman (Michigan), Ted Routi (Siena.) And whoever wins the goalie job. Tomorrow we will single out the youngsters who played well and let them lead calisthenics.

The press came to the practice for a preseason look. We downplayed expectations, never mind our lifetime numbers. Those were other boys, other opponents. Each year is a separate affair. I go to my clichés: "We'll be "okay." We're "going to stick together and battle." When the kids faced the reporters the offense praised the defense, and the defense praised the offense. Nobody bragged. Nobody better brag, either. I hate to give the opposition ammunition, and I don't care for eating crow.

March 12

We cut our squad to 40 boys today, more than I like to keep, but there were many good players we couldn't leave behind. We had one boy who was borderline score five goals in an intra-squad scrimmage the last day to earn a spot on the team. Talk about performing under pressure. This is the high school equivalent of Q-School for pro golfers. Your career can end at any moment.

Nine younger brothers made this team. Two boys have fathers who played here. Three cousins are on the team together. And we are more blue-collar than usual, the sons of cops, firemen, teachers, salesmen and small business owners. We have a few wealthy parents, but not the majority. And we have good athletes, in spite of the myth that at Ward Melville it's all about a mysterious "system," that any six clowns can play the "Backer D." (Making our team this year are five basketball players from our playoff team, one All-State soccer player, one All-County wrestler, one All-State swimmer, the usual running backs and defensive ends, and one All-League volleyball player.)

One of our boys is chronically ill, and will miss practice and perhaps some games for treatment. I don't care. His father was a Patriot. If he wasn't sick, who knows how good he would be. When he's not in the hospital, we want him with us. I have a role for him. Before the big games, when the coaches are done blabbing, he will get in the center of our huddle and give the players-only speech. No starter will take the field uninspired, you can bet on that.

Seniors get first crack at the starting line-up, the first chance to prove they can make the plays that allow us to win at the highest level. If they falter, and some will, the best juniors get their chances, and so on. We kept one sophomore on the varsity, Ryan Kunkel, the third Kunkel brother at Ward Melville. He's little physically, but may have the best stick in school, the most accurate if not the hardest shot. Alex Blechman, Nick Ward, and Kevin Kelaher have the hardest shots. But they need time and room. Little Kunkel can squeeze it past your ear, if he can take the pounding he'll get from the brute defensemen at West Islip and Smithtown and Sachem. I have to decide where to play Ward, at attack or midfield. Nick had a fast start last year at attack and suffered an ankle injury that wrecked his season. He didn't gripe or get down on himself. He got in the weight room and made himself stronger. In the summer Nick went to the Top 205 camp, made the All-Star team and earned himself a slot at the University of Maryland, his first choice. This year he'll switch positions and be one of our best middies, like his brother Mike, now at Duke. Alex Blechman is a slim, fast athlete who can shoot on the run. Josh, the goalie, is his twin. Their Dad was an All-American goalie from Freeport High School.

I invited the boys we cut to visit my office, to see what we can do for those who wish to continue playing with the team at summer camp, or in the Three-Village league. I keep those conversations private, but they are gut wrenching. Tommy O'Connor is a great kid and superior student but only an average athlete who loves to play lacrosse. Today he made the tough choice to play a second season with our junior varsity rather than quit the game. I was very proud of him; I know this wasn't easy. Tom will take one more year to improve and try to make our varsity next year, his senior year, and I'll be rooting for him, on guts alone.

We are booked to scrimmage the Comsewogue Warriors on Saint Patrick's Day. They are ten minutes away, a successful program from a smaller-school conference. Last year they went 17-1 and were ranked 55th in US. Last year we went a disappointing 13-5 and were ranked # 69. They will be sky-high for us. We sneak up on nobody. They used to call us the Green Machine, but not so much lately. We might intimidate some teams with our record. Comsewogue won't be one of them.

At a team meeting that afternoon we talk to the boys about the college recruiting process and the importance of grades and taking difficult courses and avoiding drugs and alcohol and run-ins with the police. They have so much to lose now, and so much to gain. One slip-up, one bad choice and a good kid can be ruined. Most of the juniors on this team getting "looks" have top-flight grades, which makes the process easier for them. Our guidance counselors are practiced at this, getting college coaches the paperwork they need, when they need it. As a placement service, this program is hard to beat. For thirty-something years we have sent boys off to the finest schools in the land, and those boys have distinguished themselves. There's a reason those coaches come back to Ward Melville for more.

March 13

The survivors of the final cut looked ready to work hard, so we obliged them, teaching teamwork, how much easier it is to score when we move the ball unselfishly, when you get the defense running, giving up position to chase sticks, or cheating on slides, or ball watching. I howl at them when they make the wrong choice. I want my voice ringing in their heads.

At the other end, I want us to play position-defense. We move our feet and protect the crease. I'm not a fan of dazzling take-away checks, the over-the-head and behind-the-back swipes the boys love, even though we've had our share of great pickpockets. Jon Fox (North Carolina), Harold Drumm

(UMass), Chris Passavia (Maryland) and Matt Grosso (Brown) come to mind. That's fine if we're behind late in the game and need the ball. As a general practice, though, give me guys who can run and hit and don't get beat and can handle the pole like a short-stick. At some high schools, defense is an afterthought, where you play if you're not very good. At Ward Melville, it is a marquee position. We have frequently taken good middies and made them defensemen and been very happy with the result. I always remember that the great LSM Corey Harned from Johns Hopkins played attack at Sachem—and was one of their program's all-time leading scorers.

We're a physical team, but not in the sense that we throw our bodies all over the field like idiots. We scrap for ground balls. We knock you down on the crease if you get off a shot. But we play more with our feet and our sticks than our bodies. We try to stay out of the penalty box.

We start every practice with static stretching, high-knee walking and butt kicks and side steps, working on mobility. We do individual drills and group drills. I like the basic groundball drill run real hard, because possession is so important. We do a box-out drill, a partner scooping drill, pass-and-return, tons of dodging and shooting, and catching and shooting. Tons of shooting, period. Later in the season we'll work every day on our extra-man offense and man-down defense, our riding and clearing, and face-offs.

At the end of the day we scrimmage for a while to see if the work is paying dividends. We are thorough and we prepare. Practice lasts three hours, six days a week. And then the players lift weights on their own during the season, enough so they don't wear down or get injured.

March 17

Comsewogue's new turf was slick and cold and the bus was late, but at least we got some work done, and identified some problems. (Working in the gym just doesn't do the job.) I was surprised by a lackluster effort by our first middies, except Mazzone did a nice job facing-off. A lot of standing around the restraining line waiting to rip risers into their goalie's stick, which is basically a turnover. Can't anybody shoot a bounce-shot or pick up a ground ball? Good Lord, we have to go over this stuff every year, even with seniors.

Our veteran attack throws the ball into traffic, usually without a purpose. Joey Giardinello (Suffolk CC) has to recognize who is open and who is not open, and wait for the second cutter, or the third, if that's what it takes. Giardinello was All-County last year and has been on the varsity since his freshman year. He has great wheels and a wicked left-hand, not so much of a right. I wish I could get him to care about schoolwork more than he does because he has a great opportunity here.

There was not much today of Mazzone or Alex Blechman dodging from the top, causing slides, something we've practiced ad nauseum. No movement without the ball, away from the ball, hard cuts that make a defensemen lose sight of people, cuts that create the chaos that allows easy goals. We lob the ball around flat-footed and don't meet the passes. How many balls barely made it to the receiver? How many balls got dropped? Nobody has their feet set to shoot before they catch the ball. Nobody offers a scoring threat. Nobody dodges with a purpose. Our fundamentals are pre-season sloppy and casual. We are a long way from Ward Melville lacrosse and I tell them so, angrily.

I can see right away that we won't win a thing if we coast. We are easy to guard if we don't hustle. Kelaher could be a monster with some more experience on the crease. He has that fast first step, good hands, great strength and toughness and he can shoot rockets. Kevin just needs to come overhand with the ball to improve his accuracy.

The defense will firm up nicely when DeVore returns to action, and we can attack the other guy's offense more by doubling, make them sorry they have the ball. We'll get good hustle by the defensive middies, long-poles and short, lots of ground balls. Not too many kids can run past our very fast short-stick defensive midfielders Keegan Blaney (Marist) or Nick Tsouris (Yale,) but they're small and thin, so a lot of teams are going to try. Blaney comes from a large lacrosse family, and has been raised to play the game. Tsouris, the fastest boy on the team, is the son of a doctor and a nurse and is a brilliant student, already working on college-level math. His classmates will vote him Best Dresser in the Yearbook.

The goalies played okay, all five of them, no one great. It's the offense that was crummy. And it wouldn't kill us to knock a few more people to the ground. Riding back to Ward Melville on the crowded bus at dusk I can see the boys are disappointed in themselves. That's fine. Let them remember how good West Islip and Northport will be, how hungry Yorktown is to kick our tails. Tradition cuts both ways; and we have a lot of bitter rivalries. My assistant coach Kurt Ferraro (whose sons Shane and Cole have already played for us) is going up and down the aisle patting the boys on the back, keeping their spirits up.

I look over at Maurer, who is such a gamer, and he is livid, fuming at our performance. We have a lot of work to do before Saturday when we travel to adjacent Nassau County to scrimmage Chaminade, last year's 12th ranked team in the nation.

March 18

Before practice this afternoon I catch one of our stars under a stairwell in a lip-lock with a cheerleader. I pry them apart and threaten to tell their mothers.

During practice we work on passing, catching, stick protection drills. And conditioning. You can't trust high school boys to do enough on their own. Sorry. I've learned.

While the boys are running I can see parents sitting in their cars in the parking lot, watching practice, charting their child's playing time, probably thinking their kid hasn't been treated fairly, and that I'm too hard on the boys.

After practice I drove home in the darkness pondering the make-up of the team, our strengths and weaknesses. I want the right boys in the right combinations—feeders with shooters, each lefty with a pair of righties who can finish. I'm thinking of moving some juniors ahead of some seniors and I want to be sure it's warranted, that the juniors are better, not just equal. I know what it means for a senior to see his chance at playing time evaporate. I know how it can affect morale.

At night when I get home I'd like to bounce this stuff off someone knowledgeable, but my marriage to the mother of my children ended a few years back, and my home-life is quiet now, and sometimes lonely. Honestly, there are days I wish I had someone to talk to, and days I'm glad I don't. Still, alone, I obsess about winning the league, the county and the state. We might have enough talent to go the whole way if we stay healthy and lucky. So I plot. I scheme. I call Jimmy Kaspar, another lifelong lacrosse coach. I know almost anything I say about anything, he'll disagree with.

March 19

Finally, we get a nice sunny day in a great high school stadium in Mineola. Jack Moran is a terrific coach whose wife is our Ward Melville school nurse. His Chaminade players are always D-1 studs, headed off to Princeton, Georgetown, Duke, Maryland, and Yale. Chaminade has been practicing outside for three weeks and it shows, though we play better than we did at Comsewogue. Jared Blechman scores an unassisted goal against one of their Empire defenseman. But one of our seniors doesn't hustle on a groundball, and should have been sat down for sulking after I yelled at him. Kelaher scored a few goals. He gives us so much with his physical talent and he can play almost any position on the field. Kevin is bright, with excellent grades, and played the lead in his junior high play. His brother Ryan was an All-American defenseman for us, now starting for Hofstra.

The midfield defense by our seniors is poor, like it's not part of what they do. Juniors Mike Droesch, Dominick Belvedere, and Tsouris play much harder than the starters—except for Mazzone, who always plays hard. Belvedere is small but tough, a wrestler on the Ward Melville varsity since seventh grade and closing in on membership in the Century Club for 100 career wins. Droesch is the son of two doctors, and a good student who wants to be a marine engineer. He always gives a huge effort, and is a good example to the others.

Josh Blechman was good in goal. But Maurer re-injured his shoulder trying to score, of all things, joining DeVore on the disabled list. This is driving me crazy. I want my Empire defensemen on the field. I want to see what my team looks like. John Jay is coming for a scrimmage on Wednesday, and last year they were ranked 10th in the nation.

We decide to give the boys Sunday off. Quite a few are limping as they get off the bus. You can push a team too hard, I've learned. You can push a team right over a cliff. They need rest and recovery and will bounce back rejuvenated.

I need to remember that sometimes I want to win more than they do, that they have more going on in their lives. I don't think any of them would tell you this part of the season is much fun right now. They go home and put on ice bags and wonder if I'm crazy. They nap. They have their girl friends bring them piles of food and rub their backs.

March 22

I liked the way we looked in our pre-game work, in our seven-lines drill, which is four lines of offensive players versus three lines of defensemen. The offense hunts for the open man and a good shot. Defense looks to steal or knock down the passes, and slide in time to force turnovers.

I think the pieces of our team are starting to fall into place. We saw improvement in almost all phases of the scrimmage today against John Jay.

The opponent was not as strong as our first two scrimmages, but I sense us coming together. The rest and recovery was a good idea.

Our primary need is still for a right-handed attackman who can create on the dodge and score. Jared had a bit of a setback today. Our sophomore Kunkel has the right tools and the right genes but is still overwhelmed with the size of the players and the speed of the game. So far junior Alex Beltrani has not shown me enough enthusiasm to claim the position. He's small and strong and has great quickness, but I need more vocal leadership from this position. We were also happy with Ryan Duggan in his first varsity experience. Duggan is a big lefty who will ultimately win the heated race for Class Clown in the yearbook. He has a smooth stick and will see action this season. Ben-Eliyahu was solid handling the ball, and making feeds.

But our best returning guy at attack is having all sorts of problems. Joey Giardinello remains in a deep slump and can't seem to snap out of it. He has been placed on second team for a disciplinary reason that I will keep private.

We were finally happy with the play of our two midfield units today. We switched around Kelaher and Alex Blechman to give us better balance, and I think it might work, plus it sure got the team's attention. They ran the field well, played defense, scored nine goals, and went after ground balls hard. The John Jay coach made specific mention of how hard we went after ground balls. It was good to hear since we have been emphasizing ground balls since Day One.

Our face-off work improved. Kelaher did an outstanding job at the X, as well as scoring 4 goals, putting on a show for the Hofstra assistant who scouted both teams. That's right—our scrimmages get scouted. Our defense gave a solid effort with contributions from the seven main long-poles. I have been very pleased with the play of senior Matt Rahner (University of Rhode Island) in the absence of DeVore. He has made few mistakes. Sam is back on a limited basis. When he is fully healthy and ready to go 100%, we will be stronger. We could do a better job of communicating on defense, which is funny. They are all such loudmouths off the field.

Josh Blechman (Virginia Military Institute) had a good game today in goal, stopping the ball and clearing. Ian Pennington (United States Air Force) was just OK, not as sharp as in practice. They are waging an interesting fight for the top spot. Chris Simonin had to miss the day due to a death in the family. We hope to get him some work this Saturday. Simonin's Dad played for me back in the Seventies.

I wish the weather would cooperate. It is hard to improve working indoors. We make great strides whenever we can get outdoors and work on a full field. And it stinks not being able to practice Thursday and Friday this week because of Easter. Things are coming together and we have to take time off. We need every practice we can get if we hope to beat the "big boys" later on in the season. These guys don't learn what they need to know by accident.

March 23

We got a bad break today. Middie Brian Smith (Lehigh) rolled his ankle in gym class playing European Handball. It's swollen and purple and looks like he'll be out awhile. I'm considering senior Mike Brous (Penn) and Tsouris as replacements on the second line. I'm leaning toward Tsouris on the basis of better defense and blazing speed.

The good news is Giardinello came alive in practice today, hustling, feeding, riding, and scoring. I had another private talk with him in school today, and he responded in a positive manner. He said he had lost his confidence and is feeling the pressure. I told him to relax and play the game. He's been doing this for years. He could do this in his sleep.

Now I need to find a way to get more passion from Beltrani, because I think he can play at this high level, too, and if I can get them both clicking—look out. Our sophomore Kunkel had another good practice today, scoring 3 or 4 goals. He's making the adjustment from junior high to varsity, but it's a big jump all at once.

Good to see Sam DeVore finally out on the field with fellow close defenders Maurer and Kresse while Westermann runs long-pole with senior Ted Routi. Josh Blechman had another good day in goal. He seems to be separating himself from the pack, with Pennington a close second. We will be fine with either one in goal. What a luxury.

March 24

We cancel the scrimmage-tournament scheduled for Saturday due to atrocious field conditions. This is so frustrating. We're starting to make real progress and we get hit with an injury and rotten weather. We are able to schedule some work with Comsewogue again on Monday because we need to be outdoors on a full field.

We have a busy week coming up with Shoreham-Wading River on Thursday and the Louis Acampora Tournament on Saturday. Our Division I opener is approaching and the boys need to be physically and mentally focused to meet these challenges. We're going to push them even harder in practice this week to see who has the "right stuff."

Inside Lacrosse Magazine ranks us preseason at #14 in the nation. I don't know if we're that good, or not, but we don't need anybody getting a big head. This is no time for celebrations or self-congratulations.

March 27

Easter Sunday. The weather is bad again, and our play-date with Comsewogue may fall through. Comsewogue knocked off Smithtown 6-5 to open their non-league season on Saturday. That will give them a boost of confidence. Manhasset was ranked #1 in the nation to open the season but they have already lost the Woodenstick Classic, the oldest schoolboy rivalry in the nation, to Garden City. This year the race for the mythical national championship could be wide open. I would love for us to be in it. If our defense can be as good as I think . . . .

March 29

More bad weather rolls over Long Island and we're back in the gym. Meanwhile, Huntington beats Smithtown by two in a non-league game. They've got some players at Huntington and might have a huge year: Scott Kocis, headed to Duke. The Bratton twins headed to Virginia. Zach Howell of Duke. Austin Carino. I'd take them all to play here.

At practice I notice my big-deal defense still wants to throw take-away checks and I throw my hat on the ground and howl at them. I want my defense to play defense. Run with their men. Poke, slap, lift. Knock down passes. Clear the ball. They think they know more about lacrosse than me. Just like every year.

I rip them to remind them I'm still here.

March 30

We get outside on a cold and sunny day and we run the "West Point Drill" that coach Bill Martens brought with him when he joined our staff in 1974 after years as the head coach at Half Hollow Hills. Bill didn't know where the name came from, and the guys up at West Point said they've never heard of it when I asked them. That's how old Bill is. It works wonders for conditioning. The drill is ten laps around the playing field. First one is a jog, followed by ten pushups. The next eight laps are done by sprinting the length of the field and jogging the width, each lap followed by ten more pushups. Sometimes we double it, go two laps and then do twenty pushups. Sometimes we triple it and then do thirty pushups at once. The last lap we sprint all the way around the field and finish with ten pushups.

We break up and do our practice drills, working on technique now that we're tired. We teach the sticks to be vertical, to throw and catch "in the box," up by the ear. To "look the ball into your stick." To shoot the ball overhand. None of this winding up and missing sidearm crap. Ben-Eliyahu (Wesleyan) has such good fundamentals and he's so tough in traffic. He's going to be big for us this year.

We are getting ready for the Acompora Tournament at Northport, where we will scrimmage Manhasset and Garden City, though the News 12 weatherman predicts monsoons for the weekend. We scrimmage Shoreham-Wading River tomorrow, a team that should be a county contender in the C Class. They are coached by a Ward Melville guy, Tom Rotanz, an All-American defenseman for me. I told the boys we wouldn't run "tens" after practice today, and then changed my mind at the end, to watch them handle disappointment, thinking they were done, then finding they have to push on. Good practice for overtime games.

Back in the real world, Comsewogue beats Sachem East in overtime. Pat Perritt (Syracuse) has three goals, Anthony Basciano (Penn State) has two. But Sachem North gets crushed by a good Class B team (Rocky Point) 14-2. I guess that district split really hurt them. Of course, they'll play like champs against us.

March 31

Another nice day out, although it gets cold standing around when the sun drops below the tree line. We've still got competition for jobs on attack and in the goal. I like to make them all feel like they're about to get benched and see how they respond when the screws get tight.

Our defense smothers young Shoreham-Wading River 9-2. Much better positioning, less crazy ginzu checking. Pennington was brilliant in goal. Josh was just okay. Maurer was a monster in one-on-one coverage and groundballs, but he's got to stop running up to play attack. It hurts his bad shoulder to shoot. Shoreham-Wading River is young and rebuilding. Rotanz tells me they got pounded in a scrimmage yesterday by West Islip, so we don't get too excited.

Our sophomore Kunkel played well, moving the ball, scoring a few goals. Ben-Eliyahu shot the ball well, and fought for grounders. Giardinello is the guy the other schools know about and try to shut down, and so far, their plans are working. Duggan worked at the lefty spot again today and threw some nice feeds but he needs to move his feet faster. Senior Matty Preuss (Washington and Lee) hustled hard today, but was shaky with his stick. He's a great kid, but struggling, and I feel for him. This game came so easily to his older brothers Derrick (Virginia) and Ryan (Towson.) Our senior middies are getting themselves ready, playing like they ought to, but we miss our lefty rifle Brian Smith. We were lackadaisical in spots, but not so bad. Kresse fell asleep once and I was going to yell but I saw he was already yelling at himself and ready to break his own pole over his head so I saved my breath.

That night I spoke to the Northport coaches by phone. The Acompora scrimmages are on unless we get blasted with a monsoon. They've got donated food on hand, tents erected, teams coming from out of state. Unless there is hail and lightning, we're on. That's good, I think. Harden us up against #1 Manhasset in the mud. Because we are not ready yet to play Ward Melville lacrosse, which to me is tenacious defense, smart fast breaks, the ball zipping around the perimeter, cutters streaking, the extra pass, pump-fakes, pinpoint shooting. We've shortened the bench some now, getting the most reps to the boys who will need them next week.

April 1

Many of the boys limp through practice. We push them hard here at Melville. That's not really a trade secret. They run a lot. Not just the West Point drill. Wind sprints. Mile runs. Then we scrimmage. Unless you're one of our boys with a medical condition, you better hustle your tail. We do push-ups and sit-ups, too. Tons of them. We do not get tired and break down in the fourth quarter. For most of the last thirty-five years, Ward Melville has owned the fourth quarter. Ask Sachem or West Genny or Yorktown or Northport how many times they thought they had us beat and then didn't. If I have any legacy here, it will be hard work and come-from-behind victories and the two have a lot to do with each other. I think our guys have done well in college over the years because we toughen them up here.

April 2

You see the LA-12 banner everywhere in lacrosse these days, the number young Louis Acompora wore before he was killed by a shot in the chest when he was a ninth grade goalie for Northport. Drew Thompson wears #12 at Virginia for Louis. You see LA 12 printed on T-shirts and baseball caps and tattooed on calf muscles wherever you find lacrosse players. Years ago we used to teach defensemen to "get big" in front of shooters, to block high shots with their bodies. Now we teach them, when they've done all they can to break up the play, to duck so the goalie can see the ball and make the save. There are defribulators at every game and every practice in New York State because of Louis and the charity born in his honor. I love the brotherhood we draw from this. Good teams from the tri-state area converge on a Saturday morning to play a series of 1-hour scrimmages, then eat lunch together and hang out for a while.

"Louis just loved to play lacrosse," his father says as he addresses the teams at lunch, and I start tearing up already. "Just like you boys, it was who he was. A day like this, he'd be the first one at the high school to get himself dressed and ready to go."

You can hear a pin drop as he urges them to play fair and cleanly, to take care of each other, to learn CPR, and to appreciate how lucky they are to be who they are.

After his talk, I tell our guys, one by one during the day, to go over and personally shake the hands of Louis' parents and thank them for everything they've done for our sport when they could have just curled up with grief. I want them to always know that an appreciation for their son lives on in the lacrosse players at Ward Melville.

Today, on the playing field, I expected the worst, and got the best. I mean, we were terrific. The guys played good team lacrosse, they played with determination and pride. If they can continue to improve, there is a future for us. I'm wondering if our increased running in practice has anything to do with our improvement. Actually, I'm not wondering at all.

Of course, two seniors not showing up for the bus is the stuff that drives me crazy. And just when Giardinello was turning the corner. As of now, both players are suspended for the first game. It would have to be a damn good excuse for me to change my mind. "I was sick," won't do it. My message to them will be: "You need us more than we need you". I don't want anyone around who refuses to get with the program and give total dedication.

Anyway, in the rain and mud and wind "our starters" beat "their starters" from top-ranked Manhasset first, and then Garden City. We showed intensity, pride, hitting and hustling. Brian Smith is back from his ankle injury and when we needed his left-handed shot it was there. Kelaher, Mazzone, Blechman, and Ward dominated the more-famous Nassau County boys. Our defense was alert and athletic, even in the mud.

Are we this good, I wondered? Even better than I thought? Or is Nassau County over-rated this year?

We will rest on Sunday. Practice Monday. Tuesday is our Division opener, at home. Always a day filled with anxiety and uncertainty. I believe we are ready, but you never know until the whistle blows. I'm feeling good about our midfield, our defense, and our goalie situation. Our attack is a work in progress. I'm told Northport played poorly and Sachem East played well at the scrimmages. Things to file away.

April 4

Giardinello and his partner in crime say they were sick, and that's why they missed the morning bus to Northport. So they are suspended from Game One for not informing me that they would miss the bus. No more Mr. Nice Guy. Both of them can be replaced.

Our boys hold the first pasta party of the season at the Ben-Eliyahu house. I hear Jason's mother has been cooking all day. Dianne Ben-Eliyahu is our team mother in 2005, in charge of the care and feeding and electronic communication with forty wayward boys. They tell me she's hot, so I yell at them to be respectful. The pre-game pasta party has been a feature of our program since the Eighties. Every night before a real game, the team eats dinner together. The parents rotate hosting the events, picking out their dates at the beginning of the season. The guys stuff their faces and play horseshoes and badminton. It builds team spirit and camaraderie, especially for the newcomers.

#

Before the first real game, you don't know what you have going for the long haul, not even when you've coached as long as I have. I imagine my best players suddenly having girl problems, driving difficulties, academic worries. I see them distracted, dopey, falling in love. Or some poisonous parent sews the seeds of unhappiness because he thinks his boy didn't get a decent chance. So many things can de-rail a team. I imagine Floyd's star middie Andrew Miller (Johns Hopkins) winning all the face-offs. Dodging and scoring. Through our double team, then a triple team. Passing to a guy like Justin Bunton who can also find the net. Everybody has an excuse. Everybody is yelling at each other. The boys will have a hard time sleeping tonight.

We think we have a solid line-up in place, better on defense than offense but solid throughout. We have depth. We have to use that depth. We have to build that depth with playing time for the reserves where we can, when we have a lead. I've been told I'm too slow to pull my starters. So I'm working on that. I just hate to give back wins. In fact, I can't remember any games we ever lost because I pulled my starters too soon. We used to be accused of running up the score, too, but we were just playing lacrosse, trying to get better for when we faced the better teams. I never let them score over twenty goals on anybody, even if they could. I'm friendly with those other coaches. I know those other players have feeling, too.

2005 Regular Season

April 5

Opening Day is a sunny sixty degrees at the 4PM game time. Four hundred people are ringed around the field known as Guam (because of its great distance from the building). Some smell an early-season upset. But over the years we have lost only two games on this field, one to St. Anthony's and one to West Islip. I'd be surprised if we lost our third today. Just a hunch.

The plan for covering Miller is to rotate long poles on him, starting with Maurer, then switching it up. Give him a different look each possession, a fresh opponent. Force him to work hard on defense. Limit his touches by locking him out. Tire him out. Make the other Colonials beat us. We know how to do this. We've faced great players before. Frank Urso of Brentwood and the University of Maryland was a special player, so we'd just tell our best player at the time, Kevin Boland, (Johns Hopkins,) "If Frank Urso goes to the bathroom, go with him." Or we'd run our famous zone. We've had such talented defensemen lately, we haven't bothered to teach the Backer D. Plus, it gets them ready for college to play a lot of man-to-man. Sometimes people come in with odd schemes against us, usually some kind of circle offense without a crease-man. Some teams pack six defenders down low and force us to squeeze the ball into the net. It usually doesn't work, if we can be patient.

Ultimately, on this day Miller can't outrun a rotation of Maurer, DeVore and Westermann. Short sticks Kelaher and Ward hang tough with him, too, and he only scores one goal, and that while we have two men in the penalty box. Jared Blechman, Ben-Eliyahu, Ward and Kunkel each score a pair of goals. Kelaher wins eight of nine face-offs and scores a goal. Duggan plays well in place of the suspended Giardinello, and we win 11-3. A good start for us, and not the early upset of Ward Melville some other programs wanted.

As we walk off the field I see my good friend Bob Hartranft from Nassau County Class A Champion Farmingdale in the stands, scouting us. We face them Saturday in a cross-county double-header, the Four-Star Classic. He has three terrific kids at attack, so we will adjust accordingly. One of our longtime Dads, Bob Walker, is at the game. Three of his sons played at Ward Melville, and two were All-Americans. Chris Walker (North Carolina) runs the Alumni Association with Bob Betcher (Ohio Wesleyan.) It's always great to see the Patriot family show up at the games, home and away. Newsday talks to our kids after the game and gives us a big write-up with pictures, which only fuels our opponents' animosity. At least nobody says anything stupid this year.

April 6

We wake up ranked #13 in the nation in the coach's poll. I give the boys a day off so we can practice on Sunday. (Only six days-a-week of practice are allowed during the regular season for some crazy reason. Seven during the playoffs, thank goodness.) We have other games to play before we tackle Sachem East, but we need time to get ready for Pat Perritt (Syracuse), who presents an even greater challenge than Andrew Miller. Perritt is an equally great athlete and a better lacrosse player, the top recruit in the country, and Perritt has more help. The boys have a pasta party at Mike DeSimone's house.

April 7

Longwood High School is good in so many sports. I'm just grateful lacrosse isn't one of them. Duggan starts at attack, but doesn't press his advantage, so in the second quarter Giardinello escapes my doghouse and hustles his brains out. Man, he can play when he wants to. Westermann finds him with a long clearing pass and Giardinello spins left and buries his first goal of the year. He looked more relieved than happy as he raised his stick. Our bench goes wild for him. It seems like everybody's rooting for him.

April 8

Our first junior makes his college choice when Westermann commits to follow a long line of Patriots to Brown University. (Off the top of my head, Mike Monfett, Matt Grosso, Greg Cattrano, Jed DeWick and Nicky Gentilesco all went to Brown and loved it.) When I was asked about

Westermann, I told Brown coach Scott Nelson that Jake would be an excellent player in the Ivy League. Nelson spoke to the Sachem coaches and the Northport coaches, to get opponents' points-of-view. They must have said nice things because the offer came early—as these things do nowadays. I see lots more D-1 players coming from this junior class. DeVore is likely to be an All-American and is a very good student who has already turned down Ivy offers, hoping to go to a top five lacrosse program, either Hopkins or Duke or Virginia. Kresse, Kelaher, Duggan, Tsouris, Droesch, Pat Nagel, Jon Ferro and Alex Beltrani are all juniors capable of that level of play.

April 9

We get a gorgeous day at Farmingdale High School for the Four Star double-header. Massapequa beats Sachem East 10-8 in the opener with a good crowd on hand. Lots of college scouts and high school coaches are there with clipboards. We give them something to think about as we jump out fast on a good Farmingdale team and they never catch up. Alex Blechman scores a pair. Ward notches two. Middies Brian Smith and Keegan Blaney each get one. Giardinello had a goal and three assists. We coast to a 12-5 win on some very nice team defense and good goaltending by Pennington.

April 10

Newsday makes us a big story again, but we tamp down expectations. The guys did a great job yesterday in all phases. This Nassau game is a game that we have always used as a barometer of our progress. So I would say we're on the road to bigger and better things. We just need to stay focused and play TEAM ball. We go right back to work tomorrow to prepare for Perritt and Co. This game against my close buddy Rick Mercurio's team always ties my stomach in a knot. More one-goal games than you can imagine over the years. Tough battles, some at night, played with intensity and good sportsmanship that didn't always translate into the stands, where there would be large drunken crowds and occasional partisan rumbles.

April 11

We come out totally flat at Sachem East and put ourselves in a huge hole. I can't believe the lousy first-half passing and catching, which sometimes plagues us. We go 1 for 20 on first-half shots, trying to be too fine, picking corners and posts and shooting sidearm when wide swaths of netting looked available to me. We had some mental screw-ups by our goalie, who feels awful about it, but we stick with him. Ian's earned a chance to blow a few, but his confidence is fragile, so I'm worried about how he reacts. Steaming mad at our poor fundamentals, I told the boys at halftime: "Congratulations, boys. You've got us in a dogfight now."

It got worse before it got better. We were actually down 7-2 at the start of the fourth quarter. The Sachem fans were hooting and hollering and heckling, laughing at our nationally ranked team. "Over-rated," chants rang down on our heads.

Our players were furious with themselves. Our fans were stone quiet. In the huddle assistant coach Derek Kunkel looked at our guys and snarled: "You get your heads up right now. Do you hear me? We don't lose like this to Sachem. We're coming back to win this f . . . ing game starting right now, you understand me? You're going to talk about this f . . . ing game for the rest of your lives. Now, let's go."

Our boys believed him because Derek had been there. You could sense the change in attitude. Then Giardinello gets us going with a quick goal on a dodge from X, and you could see our boys come alive. Bang, bang, bang, bang. Every face-off goes our way. Every shot goes in. Kelaher ties it. Ben-Eliyahu puts us ahead. We get great defense by Maurer and the juniors down the stretch, forcing turnovers, stealing passes, digging out ground balls, only to watch our attack give it right back. I almost keeled over from the tension. Perritt, desperate, puts down his short stick and picks up a pole to try to force a turnover. And he does it!

There was a moment in the fourth quarter when Maurer allowed Perritt to get off a couple of outside rockets that just missed. So I told Andrew to get up close on his hands. Andrew stands up and looks at me and says, "We can give him these or we can give him layups." I told Maurer to keep doing what he was doing. With three seconds left in the game, they have the ball behind our cage, and everyone from Melville thinks it's over except Pennington and Westermann. We've got guys dancing and high-fiving and hugging at midfield, while Westermann, screaming for help, is alone with three Arrows lined up in front of our cage like a firing squad. The ref puts the ball in play for a quick re-start, the Sachem East attacker feeds an open man. And Ian stones him high from three yards away. The horn blows. Our guys at midfield go, "Huh? What?"

Call it the great escape of 2005. Giardinello has four goals and two assists, a monster fourth-quarter effort. We hold Perritt to a two goals and one assist. Driving home that night, all I can think is we played awful lacrosse for three quarters and still won on the road. Let's hope we learned something. It was certainly a gut-check. I think we've got something going on this year. It's a completely different ballgame if we bury a few shots in the first quarter. Shooting 1 for 20 is not going to get it done against anybody really good. Still, it could have been worse. We could have lost our first game.

April 13

We bounced back from our shaky visit to Sachem East with a solid 16-1 romp over a young Bay Shore team to move to 5-0. Everybody played in the game because we want everyone improving, not just the starters. Ward, Giardinello, Ben-Eliyahu all nail hat-tricks. Kunkel scores again. Mike Droesch buries his first career varsity goal for us on a top-shelf bouncer. Our three goalies allow but one goal. The win today put our career record at 670 wins, 68 losses, pretty much a 10-1 ratio over the years. We once had a 71-game winning streak that was broken by West Genesee in the New York State championship game.

We are looking forward to our annual intersectional game with Hudson Valley powerhouse Yorktown this Saturday. I always see this game as another opportunity for us to grow. This rivalry began in 1974 when a young middie named Keith Blaney moved to the Three Villages and joined our team. He told me that the place he moved from played lacrosse much as we did, that we should challenge his old friends at Yorktown. So we called them up and made a date to play at West Point. Our young knuckleheads thought we we're going upstate to bounce around some apple-knockers, so they had themselves a big party the night before the game. We lost decisively and a rivalry was born.

Before practice today I learned that Pennington, who struggles to stay confident, has taken to wearing a piece of tape on his glove, with a message to himself from his teammates. "Ian, you're the best!" it says. There are a lot of game-time rituals around here. Westermann wears the same shredded pro wrestling underwear and North Carolina fishing tournament t-shirt for every game, don't ask me why. I'm all in favor of whatever helps us win. As long as Westermann washes that stuff after every game.

April 15

After our tune-up practice and film session I watched Scotty Craig's talented West Islip team take on Sachem East. A lot of our boys also attended the night game, scouting the opposition for themselves, and I like the camaraderie, our desire and interest to be great. We sit together in the stands and watch West Islip put on a clinic. The Lions win 17-0. I mean, it's a lay-up drill. West Islip looks like Johns Hopkins. The Sachem East kids look so discouraged they may have quit on Rick. The Sachem parents were screaming at their kids, which never helps. I certainly hope West Islip isn't that good. They can't be that good. 17-0 against a team we beat 8-7. I don't think a Sachem lacrosse team has been shutout in twenty years.

Ian Pennington damn well better be the best.

April 16

On a gorgeous day for a road trip to Yorktown we are ranked #10 in the nation. For the squad's further edification I have brought along the videotape of our 1999 state championship game against upstate nemesis West Genny. Down a goal with twenty-two seconds left in the game, Ward Melville miraculously wins. After the tape ends someone mentions the year 1997 and my assistant coach Anthony Pisciotto calls out, "Best year of my life, coach. Twenty-one-and-oh. We beat Mahopac in the state championship game. Remember the score?"

I do, indeed. A gut-wrenching two-to-one win for Ward Melville.

I fear a slow start today at Yorktown because of the long bus ride, stiff legs, and nerves, and because this group starts slow normally. And we do start slowly, slipping and sliding on the brand new rug in Charlie Murphy Stadium. Our boys in football cleats have more difficulty with footing than they ever did at Stony Brook. Sneakers or turf shoes would have been better. Who knew? We trade first-half goals with Yorktown and then fall behind by a few, making them look like the All-American's some of them are. At halftime, I was about to rip them when one of the younger guys said angrily, "Okay, Melville, it's time for us to stop sucking."

I couldn't have put it better myself. So I didn't.

The second-half was all Patriots, a 10-1 explosion. I almost felt bad for Yorktown coach Dave Marr. Giardinello moved to new level of maturity and leadership today. (Seeing Duggan play his position so well probably didn't hurt.) He always had the wheels and the talent, now he has the desire. He's been with me on the varsity since ninth grade, as has Maurer. Giardinello told the Newsday reporter after the game that he's "been waiting all his life to play for a team this talented." It must feel that way to him, as if he's been on this team a lifetime. I know how he feels, only for me it actually has been a lifetime of friendships and excitement. Wait until he looks back on these years of camaraderie and achievement. It will feel like a glorious instant.

All in all, a great job. The guys raised the level of their game in the second half—great defense, unselfish offense, and everyone contributing. During the handshake after the game I heard Gary Rainiolo, a Cornhusker middie headed to Fairfield, say to one of our guys: "Wow-do you guys hustle."

Now that makes me proud.

I am developing a real liking for this group. They are positive, hard working, and fun to be around. I also get the sense that they are enjoying the season, and our chase of perfection. My only concern right now is that the team is looking past Lindenhurst to Thursday's game with West Islip. This could be a big mistake because Lindy is always athletic and they have some good lacrosse players. We need to focus on them if we want to enter the West Islip game with a clean record. There is always something to worry about as a coach of high school guys. Grades. Family problems. Girlfriends. Beer blasts. Drugs. So many things can go wrong.

But I'm looking forward to the warm weather. Our depth and conditioning become huge factors in our favor in the heat.

April 17

I played golf with Jesse Smith, our boys' basketball head coach at Ward Melville, where his sport is traditionally an afterthought, something guys do to stay in shape. Don't ask my score. My knees don't work right anymore and I'm going to have to address that. Last year's hoops team made the Suffolk County playoffs for the first time in 13 years. Beltrani made All-League at point-guard. DeVore, Tsouris and Westermann were defensive stoppers. Beltrani was unbelievable during our one playoff game as we came from 10 points down in the fourth quarter to force overtime. Alex had at least four steals in the backcourt and four assists and not until our Empire player Kellen Scantlebury fouled out in overtime was the game decided.

I find the winter of running and jumping and defensive footwork to be an advantage for them, and I know some college coaches agree. They start faster in the spring. They arrive for tryouts in good shape. They don't get early season injuries. Same thing for our wrestlers. The more sports they play the better, as far as I'm concerned, as long as their stick-work is up to par.

I imagine the boys slept late today. They don't get enough sleep because their schoolwork is so tough, lots of homework and pressure to excel, and the juniors have SAT prep courses, and driver's education.

Tomorrow we start preparations for the Lindenhurst game on Tuesday. They always bang us around for the joy of it. They have played good teams tough this year, and they will be psyched up for us. The buzz is for our game against West Islip, but we don't want to get ahead of ourselves. A lot of air leaves the balloon is we're not both undefeated on Thursday.

April 18

We hold a long hard practice of playoff quality and intensity. I want their damn attention. It's time to lock-on, to put aside all distractions and think of nothing else but winning lacrosse games. Forget the girlfriends and social life. Do your homework and play hard. It will be over before you know it. Some of our best juniors sign up tonight at East Islip High for tryouts for the Empire Team. Sam and Andrew have made it the last two years. A few of the others could join them. The pasta party is at Nick Miceli's (Kean) house. I hear the food is fantastic, but I don't go to these, as I think it is something that belongs to the boys and their parents.

April 19

It's Patriot's Day in New England, and I'm hoping it's the same on Long Island. We take a bus ride south to Lindy, expecting a physical battle. Our kids come out tough and take the hits without complaint and it's never a contest on the scoreboard. We're ahead 8-1 at the half, 14-3 at the end. Alex Blechman scores four goals, Ben-Eliyahu three. Giardinello had four assists. We play almost everybody and it's a noisy, happy bus ride home.

Now it gets serious—#1 West Islip.

We're ready. Bring 'em on.

April 20

I got an e-mail forwarded to me, about how Chris Passavia, one of our MLL pros, is pumped about the current team, and coming out to watch the West Islip game. He is happy to see a group that cares about the good name of the Green-and-Gold. Chris was on our last State Champion, the 2000 team, as special a collection of high school players as I have ever come across. Chris (Maryland) and Drew Casino (Princeton) and Nick Gentilesco (Brown), Ryan Kelaher (Hoftsra), Will O'Dwyer (Villanova), Matt Monfett (Loyola), Tom Theodorakis (Syracuse). We sent strong players from that team to play and win in the NESCAC for John Raba at Wesleyan, all over Division III. These 2000 guys are already men, finished with college, starting careers. They were boys when I had them, fun loving and blessed with great talent.

We finish installing our surprises for West Islip. New wrinkles on our rides, and we are not sliding from the crease tomorrow. Screw them. That's what they want us to do, so they can feed their big hammer Ryan Euell (Notre Dame). We are going to slide adjacent, even if it takes us longer to get there. Or not at all. We would rather have Pennington face their middies from fifteen yards out than their open attackmen from the crease. We've told our poles they can't get burned one-on-one by Matt Sullivan (Towson) or Kevin Federico (UNC) and we can't take penalties. Easy for me to say.

On offense, we want to slow things down unless we have a numbers advantage. We might be able to win a track meet with them, but I don't see the point. If this were the old NBA, they are the LA Lakers and we are the knock 'em down New York Knicks. Slow it down, make them play defense, allow no lay-ups, expect the unexpected, and fight till the end. If we can stay close, we can win it. We cannot fall behind as we have been doing.

On LaxPower they are calling this the "War on the North Shore," the biggest game of the year on Long Island. I told our guys not to buy the hype. It's a regular season division contest. Win, lose, or draw, we'll see these guys again. Just make sure you properly introduce yourself. Set the proper tone. The pasta party is at Jared Blechman's house, my gutsy little senior attack. I keep thinking Kunkel will beat him out soon, and Jared keeps playing better and better, holding off the inevitable.

As I ride east that evening I notice the trees are growing buds and the grass is getting greener. Is there a better time of year than an undefeated April? I sure don't think so, but it's not something a grown man can pray for. Tonight I have a proud, happy, nervous team. What will I have tomorrow evening? One way or the other, they'll be a little more experienced for the playoffs.

I have heard some griping about our back lacrosse field, where we are playing our home games this year, except for the Sachem North game at Stony Brook University. Actually, the surface of Guam is in good shape this year and the boys like it fine. There is only one set of single bleachers, though, so hundreds of people stand at the fence that rings the field. Tomorrow that might be a thousand. People have grown used to us playing big games in our football stadium, but that's a mess now, the track under reconstruction. Back in the 80's we played out back and we won all the time. Once, I remember, we were down 5-1 to West Islip and came back to win 7-6. I hope there is some magic left, that we have not used it up. For both teams I hope that nobody gets hurt. And I hope nobody gets humiliated. Simple as that. Play ball.

April 21

Cool. Sunny. Perfect for a game against the best. I tell the local reporters I think we might lose today, that they might be a little better than us. I'm not lowering the bar. I'm telling the truth. These guys are that good, two Empire players at attack, and one on defense.

Well, the bleachers were stuffed by three-thirty. Painted-students and lax fans three-deep ringed the back playing field. There were scouts, high school and college coaches, a taping section worthy of a Dead show. Former Patriots Derek Kunkel and Anthony Pisciotto have served as volunteer assistant coaches all year. They were joined on the sideline for this game by Boston Cannon defenseman Chris Passavia (WM 2000), who said afterward, "I couldn't be prouder of these guys for bringing the Green-and-Gold back to the top. Lots of the alums are into it this season."

Kelaher won the opening face-off, but the first few possessions for both sides went for naught as the tension mounted. Then Maurer scooped a ground ball and burst across the field, faking passes with his pole, pushing the issue until he drew a slide. Maurer fed Giardinello who buried the ball in the back of the net for the first of his two goals on the day.

Moments later Jared Blechman hustled and harassed the West Islip goalie into a turnover on a clear. Blechman grabbed the ball and fed Kelaher, who bounced it home through a tangle of legs. Blechman scored again at the end of fast break to put us on top 3-0 at the end of the first quarter. In the second quarter West Islip found its bearings, and sloppy play by us allowed the Lions a second life at 3-2.

In the third quarter Giardinello froze his man with a double-swim move and snaked his way to the net for an unassisted goal. Kunkel came off the bench to find Ben-Eliyahu alone on the crease. Meanwhile DeVore, Maurer, Kresse and Westermann and Blaney kept the clamps on the 15-goal-per-game offense. In the best one-on-one matchup of the day, DeVore shut out his LI Empire teammate Matt Sullivan.

At the beginning of the fourth quarter Kunkel picked up a loose ball rebound and notched his second goal of the day. A few minutes later Ben-Eliyahu repaid Kunkel's earlier assist with a beauty of his own to finish the Ward Melville scoring at 7. Pennington held the fort during the last few frantic minutes, with 16 saves in his finest performance to date.

I like what I see here. These boys like each other. Good teams have that. They don't get down on each other when things go wrong. And that kid Kunkel has come along. Our guys are doing a tremendous job of restoring the tradition of Ward Melville lacrosse. Our task now is to play each game as hard as we played today. We must not rest on our laurels. That will be my job. To keep on pushing.

Giardinello and Maurer are a bit banged up, not sure if they will be ready to go for a while. I'm thinking of shutting them down tomorrow so they will be ready for Northport. Speaking of Northport, I was shocked they lost to Mahopac yesterday. Hope they don't come to life against us. A win over them puts us in the driver's seat. A loss makes a very messy three-way tie for first. I don't even want to think about it.

#

I scouted the Northport at Smithtown game that night and sat with West Islip's Bill Turri, an assistant coach and a West Islip Dad. Someone walked past us and asked him if he's mad at me. I said, "Why would he be mad at me. They've beaten us the last four times." We know we'll play them again and we respect them. We know either team could win.

My scouting report has Northport looking great on offense and shaky on defense. Smithtown is tough and talented but young. Northport rattled them. Northport is Travis Burr and Craig Dowd and about ten guys named Max, all of them very good. We have a fast kid to run with each and every one of them. At least I think we do. I don't want to listen to Kaspar's crap if we don't.

Also, after much soul-searching, I have decided to retire at the end of this year from full-time teaching, but not from coaching. I'd like to stay on in that capacity for a few more years, try to win a few more big ones. I still have the energy and the fire in the belly. I'd have even more time to prepare my team. Heck, I live alone. What else am I doing? And I love this stuff. I keep the retirement news on the low-down. The last thing I want is for this year to be about me.

April 22

Earth Day. We wake up ranked #4 in the nation, so it's time to bring the boys down to earth. We're halfway through the regular season, and haven't won anything. There is more ground to cover. We run them like horses this evening. They grumble, but it's a happy grumble.

Sadly, we learn that assistant coach Derek Kunkel is leaving us, to take a full-time real job in Manhattan. (Hey, it happens) It's been great to have him on the sidelines and the boys have learned a lot from him. But I need to replace him with a high-quality assistant. When I get home I make a phone call to an old friend, one who can get up to speed in an instant: Bill Martens.

April 23

We watch game film and correct mental mistakes. Then we take them outside and run them like dogs in the mud until their tongues are hanging out. They do not bitch at all and everyone gives a good effort. They have bought into the hard work wholeheartedly. I like this team, and the way Mazzone and Maurer are leaders-by-example more than talkers. Everybody looks up to them for their ability and work ethic.

April 25

We beat West Babylon 14-4 easily on a Kunkel hat trick. Keegan Blaney gets a pair of goals. Alex Beltrani also scores a nice goal, making a case for more playing time. Brian Smith scores a goal, which I'd like to see more of. We play sloppily at times but still good enough by a lot. We empty the bench early. I love it when everybody plays. Keeps the griping to a minimum, from players and their parents.

April 26

We had a very poor practice today. They were sluggish, lazy, unfocused, and I don't know why. Sometimes it happens and we can get all over them or let it go. I'm sure they are looking forward to tomorrow and will be ready to play. But my instinct is telling me it might be time for a break. We have been going hard for the last month. If we get through this week with a clean record I'm planning on giving them the weekend off to rest and recover. It's very easy to work them too hard and peak too soon. We have a long way to go. At least I hope we'll be playing big games a month from now.

April 27

Assistant coach emeritus, and defensive genius, Bill Martens joins the team on the sideline for the Northport game. Bill was head coach at Half Hollow Hills and then my defensive assistant for over twenty years. Seeing him back, I feel like we're a couple of old gunslingers, hanging on against the youngsters. But we're crafty gunslingers. Don't count us out.

Instead of rain on this trip to Northport, we get a hot and muggy day, which is perfect for our depth. There are more Ward Melville fans at the game than Northport people, which shows what energy winning brings to a program.

Again, in the early going we start casually, throwing the ball away, or directly to wide-open Tigers. We screw up a slide, jog when we should sprint, drop passes and blow clears. Who are these guys? Some of our best athletes are so—how shall I put it? Casual. Suave. I love them as kids, but they drive me crazy as players. I want them to hustle, damn it, all the time. Like Maurer does. We are down by one (5-6) at the half, but I'm not overly worried. Somebody jokes that we've got them where we want them, because we are nothing if not a second-half team.

Kelaher wins all the third quarter face-offs and an eight-nothing explosion turns a tight game into a laugher. The Tigers are gasping for air, and we keep running and running. Our fans are going wild, so it sounds like a Melville home game. The 14-8 whipping repays last year's bad loss at our place, on a day our top defenseman Will Konczynin got so sick he couldn't play and went to the emergency room.

I feel bad for the Northport coaches Jim Kaspar and Bob Macaluso, two of my best pals, and very good men. Their team is just lopsided. Too many good athletes on one side of the field, and not enough on the other. After the game Kelaher limps onto the bus with ice strapped on his knee. Not good for us. Blaney always does a nice job on short-stick defense and facing off for us, but I want my lines intact as their chemistry improves with time. Alex Blechman scores four goals, and Ward gets two. Smith needs to be more selfish. He's supposed to make the opposition respect that lefty cutter, but he's a quiet kid who is usually content to set the pick for Alex.

He needs to assert himself more. Or Alex needs to assert himself less. We're easy to scout. Northport couldn't stop Giardinello, who had three goals and five assists. Ben-Eliyahu and Kunkel and Jared Blechman got the job done again at attack. Not big, not that fast, they just get the job done.

Meanwhile, West Islip crushes Smithtown and East Islip beats upstart Half Hollow Hills East at the buzzer. William Floyd wins again. And Lindy wins again. The positioning for playoff seeds is critical. We want the first-round bye, a chance to heal some wounds and to scout the opposition. I call for practice tomorrow at 9:30 AM, if only to limit any untoward celebrations tonight. We are about halfway to Cornell University and a championship match-up with West Genny. You don't spike the football on the fifty-yard-line, now do you? This is no time to hoist a beer, and I tell them that. I'm not sure they listen, but we try.

April 28

Coach Bill Martens arrives at practice in his 1999 State Championship hat, just to remind everyone of what we can accomplish. Bill is one of the great defensive minds in the game. He invented the Backer D, and brought the West Point drill to Melville, although the current guys at West Point tell me they've never heard of it.

The pasta party is at Blaney's house. What a lax family that is. Dad (Keith) played for me. Mom (Erin) coaches the girls' team at Ward Melville. Daughter Kelly played here and at the University of Vermont. Ryan played here and is now at Marist. Keegan is verbally committed to Marist. Sister Shaylyn may be the top recruit in the country next year and headed to Notre Dame. Deron is the baby, and she might turn out to be the best. They have a cousin, Colin Briggs, who is an All-American from Rhode Island, and a University of Virginia signee.

#

At school a little birdie tells me Cory Manning, one of our basketball stars, threw a victory party for my lacrosse team last night. LaxBash they called it. Not to be confused with KresseFest I and II. I really can't wait to thank Cory in person when I see him. (They think I don't know stuff. I know stuff. I know too much stuff.) I swear, I smell beer on anyone's breath and I will run them all into the ground.

April 29

Connetquot is smart and tough and we can't take them lightly. David DeSimone (Swarthmore) on attack, and Nick Montasero (Colgate) at face-off middie are bona-fide All-Division players. Mark Leggerio (Lafayette) is tough junior middie, headed to the Patriot league to play football. These guys want to bounce us around, and we know it. But our defense is outstanding once again. Westermann blankets their big middies and Maurer and DeVore and Kresse devour their attack. We allow only a two-man-down goal (on a stupid, self-indulgent, better-not-happen-again penalty) and a garbage goal during the late fourth quarter. Our circle offense clicks for 14 goals, spread out among the troops. Suddenly our attackers are feeding beautifully, finding the open man, hitting "the box" with their passes. Mazzone, Ward and Smith all rang the bell today. If only our middies passed as well as they shoot, we'd be unstoppable. But I can't complain. These guys have convinced me that they are pretty damn good. I didn't anticipate being 11-0 at this stage of the season. If we stay focused and work hard there is no telling how far we can go. I believe resting them this weekend will pay dividends next week. We should be refreshed, healed, and ready to go on the second half of our season.

I am so proud of our skin-tight defense and unselfish offense. These guys have really bought in to the concept of Ward Melville Lacrosse—it's a beautiful thing to watch.

April 30

While we are resting our bones, West Islip gets itself into a 16-14 shootout with a good team from Pennsylvania. And Jack Moran's Chaminade team loses by a goal to Yorktown, up there. Interesting. Chaminade beat St. Anthonys and St. Anthony's lost to #1 McDonogh by a goal, down in Baltimore. I'm not that big on comparative scores, but we belong among the elite again, is what I think, and, as always, Yorktown is improving because they have a great coach in Dave Marr.

We too have come a long way. When we began the pre-season, I had my suspicions we might be two top-of-the-line players short, but I underestimated what good kids this bunch is, and how they could make up for that with effort—and how tight they have become on this ride. Some of our seniors have suffered personal disappointments with diminished playing time as the team has matured and improved. I understand, and appreciate the good spirits they have maintained for the benefit of their teammates. But the juniors and the sophomore getting playing time of late have been better. The team is better for it. And nobody wants to lose. The town is openly in love with these kids again, and they are all little celebrities in their green-and-gold Patriots Lacrosse jackets. Please keep them healthy, and Lord, let them behave.

May 1

Manhasset handles John-Jay-Cross River, but not as easily as we did at our scrimmage. We DO belong in this conversation again. Am I convincing myself of our own merit? I don't know. We're not perfect. We have flaws. Do I always expect to win? No. But I always dread losing, that long walk back to the locker room or a quiet ride home on the yellow school bus.

May 2

I'm thinking about the young Smithtown Bulls, who were rated highly when the season began, but have dropped slightly as their youth has cost them. They did whip Massapequa early. They have a good young attack and a couple of stud middies in senior Jake Kalata and junior Brad Burton. Goalie Joe Marra is a junior and a good one. They will be excellent soon. I just hope it's not tomorrow afternoon. The Smithtown head coach Kevin Huff knows what he's doing, and these guys have beat us the last few years. A lot of people beat us. Have I mentioned that yet? That's why this season has been so satisfying.

May 3

The last few years Smithtown ran out to a big lead on us and held on for dear life. This year—missing most of its high-powered offense at game-time because they were taking AP exams—the young Bulls were the ones who quickly got in trouble. Mazzone was everywhere, and passed out an assist to just about everybody wearing green-and-gold. Ben-Eliyahu got three goals, Kunkel a pair. Blaney won-ten faceoffs in a row. Alex Blechman has become a scoring machine, cutting off the solid Smith pick. Duggan converted a nice feed from X by Beltrani, the two junior attackmen I need to click next year. A nice day for us on the back field. We held the Bulls to one second-half goal. Matt Rahner, Kresse, Westermann and goalie Pennington killed a three-man-down penalty for one minute, then Nick Micele (Kean) joined the defense to kill off a two-man down opportunity with our evil Empire Twins in the penalty box for slashing. Game over. Some days we just smother people.

William Floyd beat Sachem East in the annual Pat Perritt-Andrew Miller All-American match-up, further complicating whom we will see in the early rounds of the play-offs. Northport got killed at West Islip 16-4. I still think we'll see West Islip again in the finals, if we don't stumble. I hope those real good Northport kids haven't quit on Bob and Jim, but I have other things to worry about.

May 4

We prepare for Half Hollow Hills East, who plays this weird two-man, hold-the-ball game that has befuddled good teams this year. They've got good coaches and they've scouted us well. They know what we do and who does what. Of course, when we face off with two poles on the wings, they might be surprised. Coach Ray Weeks stopped by practice today. It's turned into old home week at Ward Melville, everybody happy we're winning.

With winning streaks, come rituals, like Ian's pre-game breakfasts with his Mom. And Ian's note to himself on his gloves. Now the whole school tells him that. Kids who don't play lacrosse pass him in the hall and say, "Ian, you're the best."

Westermann has been wearing the same pair of skanky, shredded, undefeated pro-wrestling underwear all season. He has also been wearing a t-shirt under his game jersey that commemorates his Uncle Bob Watson's fishing team in Wilmington, North Carolina. Why? I asked him. Because his Uncle Bob is battling cancer, he tells me. Oh.

The pasta party is at Mazzone's house, where Kenny is merely the oldest of five great young athletes. You just haven't met them all yet.

May 5

It was no work of art, but we won ugly on the road 7-3. Most good seasons have a few of these clunkers where we don't click, where we play like jerks. As we expected, Hills held the ball to shorten the game and kept it close. We missed too many opportunities at the offensive end. Jared Blechman hit two posts. Kunkel failed to finish a few chances, rushing.

Ben-Eliyahu got us a million groundballs, or it would have been closer. You know what? Good for them, for keeping it close, but they never tried to win. In the early fourth quarter they inverted their offense and stood with the ball at x. Westermann and their middie literally had a conversation as the clock ticked down and parents from both sides argued the strategy in the bleachers.

We killed a two-man penalty in the fourth quarter to put the game away. Ian was great between the pipes, but he's got to stop throwing the ball away on clears. Defense played well, both our long-stick middies and the close guys, also short-stick Blaney on their good dodger. We have been lucky with injuries so far, except that Maurer's shoulder has been hurting all year and will not get better. Our kids have jumped up from all the big hits, and they did so again today.

Sachem North is next. They've had a tough year by their high standards. But they'll come hard at us on Saturday night at Stony Brook University. Just because they've been split in half doesn't mean they despise us any less. It's not by accident that our closest game so far this year was Sachem East. Through the years, this has been one of the high school game's best rivalries, with a touch of class warfare. Hope it doesn't rain.

May 6

An easy day at practice. We kind of fooled around with the kids. I told them I thought we had peaked too early this year, that it was my fault, maybe I put too much emphasis on winning in the regular season, and not enough on building strength and depth with an eye toward the playoffs. I want to take some of the pressure off them. People see we're still undefeated and are starting to think big. Not me. Not yet. We have holes.

Today I bent over and picked up a lacrosse stick, which I almost never do. Why wreck the mystique? I told the boys to take a damn picture, they would never see this again. Their jaws dropped, like, "Wow. Now, I've seen everything: Cuozzo with a lacrosse stick in his hands. Somebody throw him a ball. See if he can catch it."

Back in the day, I told them, pretending to crank up a riser, I used to score from the midfield line. They started laughing and told me to try it now. I said I didn't want to hurt Ian's feelings, and they fell down laughing. Ah, winning. It does wonders for everyone, even a sixty-seven year old high school coach like me.

May 7

It's raining, hard, which could mess up our Patriots Pride double-header tonight at LaValle Stadium. Oh, we'll play, and the Field-Turf will be fine, but these kids were looking forward to a raucous, semi-full house.

Our fine girls' team takes on powerhouse Huntington (11-1) at 4 PM and we face-off at 6:30. I hope our kids don't fall asleep on this one, just because North has been down. Also, our juniors have their SATs in the morning, so they'll be mentally tired and their legs will be stiff from sitting still for hours. We'll give them extra stretching in the warm-up tonight and some extra jogging. I'd like to get a safe lead, pull my starters early and keep them rested and healthy. We'll let everybody have a nice long run before a large home crowd. They've all worked so hard. They all deserve it, and not just the starters.

St Anthony's s plays at Yorktown today. West Islip hosts Mahopac. Everybody is getting tournament-tough with no risk to their county playoff seeds. Not us. We're now playing for perfection. I'm not sure which is harder.

By game-time the rain is gone and the sun is peeking out. A steady wind dries the artificial field quickly. We draw a noisy crowd of maybe a thousand fans and after our typical slow start, we run Sachem North out of the building 14-3. A six-nothing third quarter sealed the deal. Then Kresse made a simple mental mistake, and I got on him and sat him down, and he's fuming at me the whole time, which almost made me laugh out loud. I love that big kid: He's so good, and strong as an ox, getting better all the time, pushing DeVore for "the best defenseman" on the Island and in the country, not just at Ward Melville.

Kelaher scored a couple of amazing goals on the way to a hat-trick. Kunkel keeps coming on with a pair of goals, chipping more playing time away from Jared, one of the little dramas that go on within a team inside a season. The big lead allowed us to get our bench experience in front of family and friends. Mike Droesch scored again and continues to impress me at midfield, and Vince Redko, a world history buff, played very well on defense in the second half. Got some nice work in at long-pole middie from Ferro (VMI) and senior Sean McGreevey. We win 14-3 and climb on the bus happy men. Back at the high school their rowdy friends and girlfriends are waiting for them, with parties planned.

I crossed my fingers.

May 8

On Sunday, we rested. It's Mother's Day. We have some Ward Melville boys playing in the NCAA tournament again, including three Marist kids who have to go to Homewood to play against Johns Hopkins—some reward for winning your own league. Mike Ward and Duke have a nice seed. We may see him in the Final Four, as we did last year with Chris Passavia at Maryland and Drew Casino at Princeton.

May 9

Back to work, hard, on a warm afternoon. We run Tens, as only Bill Martens can order them up. The boys don't mind. They know what all this work has got them. They are now ranked #1 on Long Island, and #3 in the nation according to Inside Lacrosse. I see them in the hallways at school with the cute girls hanging around them, and I have to break up some under-the-stairs smooching.

The guys this year have added a tradition. As the school bus pulls back into the Ward Melville driveway from a winning road trip, someone in the back asks: "Hey, Melville—who bad?" And they all cry in unison, "We bad!" And then they laugh.

After practice I gathered my four starting long-poles together and gave them a pep-talk. I told them that I'd had great individual defenders before, and they all know the names. I just couldn't remember when I'd had a unit that worked as well together and as selflessly. And three of the four come back to be seniors next year. Even so, we won't easily replace Andrew Maurer. What a player, and what a performance he has given this year, his motor always running, and he's doing it with one arm.

After practice I jumped in my SUV and went and scouted the Smithtown-Middle Country game. We play Middle Country Friday. There's another program on the rise. I'm telling you, good lacrosse is everywhere now.

May 10

East Islip has a 9-4 record, and we play them tomorrow. Everybody says they're pretty good, don't take them for granted. Like that would happen.

The pasta party is at Gerry Belvedere's tonight. I've had three of his sons on my teams, and each one was tougher than the last. Dominick has only played a little this year, but will play a lot next year. Our midfields were just so deep, tough to crack. Only Kelaher could make the leap, and thank God he did. If anyone gets hurt, though, I wouldn't hesitate to play my top three or four junior middies. They will probably all play Division I in college, and Nick Tsouris might be our best all-around player next year. How many high school coaches can say that about their bench?

May 11

We visit East Islip, with their gaudy 9-4 record. "Business trip," yells Kelaher as we climb off the bus. "Let's get 'er done."

I look in the stands and see lots of videotaping going on, and not by parents looking to shop their sons to college. Our opponents are trying to figure out how to beat us. But we don't have that many weaknesses that I can see. We jump out to a four-one start and win 14-4, an easy game after all. Kunkel scores four goals and Giardinello does, too, with five assists. It's now evident that Kunkel is ready to start for us, no matter how hard senior Jared Blechman plays. But do you change the starting line-up when your team is undefeated?

If it makes you better, you do.

Maurer blankets Brett Djaha, their Empire player and the focal point of their offense. Their frustrated parents are screaming at their kids: "Don't let them do that to you. Hit them!" Our always knowledgeable and completely reasonable parents are screaming at the referees for allowing them to foul us. At 13-2 we pull the starters, before anyone critical to our mission gets hurt. I want to see next year's team play for a while, get a feel for who needs to be tweaked, encouraged, or challenged. Tomorrow at practice we will rest the seniors, and our juniors will scrimmage our undefeated Junior Varsity. I have to say, some kids are already playing their way out of our future plans, and some other kids will barge their way in. Now is the time to produce, and I tell them so. Every day is the time to produce. It has always been that way.

After we got back to Ward Melville from our game ("We bad!") I watched that pesky Half Hollow Hills East squad upset Sachem East, throwing the playoff seeds into turmoil. Jimmy Kaspar calls me at home that night and tells me defiantly that Northport's not done yet. "Don't count us out, Joe. We're coming together."

With four future All-Americans on his roster, they should be coming together. I tell Jim that if they make the semifinals against West Islip, he can be sure I'll be rooting for him. He thinks we'd have a better chance against West Islip than his Tigers.

I think he's crazy.

This is a great time of year for the boys and me. Everything is about the green-and-gold and growing strong together. I just hope we don't trip up, or somebody does something dumb. We've come a long way, and a lot of people are watching us now.

The pasta party was at Nagle's tonight. Pat's a junior attackman who should play a lot for us next year, maybe even as a midfielder. He is always on the move, a good finisher, a good ground ball man, makes the right play, a lot like Ben-Eliyahu. His dad Rich was a goalie at Oceanside High, and a longtime coach in the Three Village system.

Tomorrow afternoon we can wrap up our first undefeated Division I Championship since the 2000 season, get a little something brand new to hang on the gymnasium wall. Anytime you win a Division championship you have to be happy. That means the job is halfway done.

2005 Playoffs

May 15

Hoping to scrimmage the Chaminade Flyers again this week, I put in a call to Jack Moran. Their excellent squad would give us a very healthy workout.

Today I saw our former goalie Mick Foley at the Special Olympics. We had a great group of Ward Melville players there to volunteer. All-American attackman Chris Ritchie from Mt. Sinai joined our guys. Kevin Federico and a gang of West Islip players worked their own booth in the Olympic Village, allowing themselves to be sprayed with hoses. You know I love these challenged children . . . and often note the irony that during the day I coach students who carry the greatest burdens, and in the afternoon I coach players given the greatest of gifts. I was very proud of our guys for giving of their time to a good cause. That was a good day.

Jack Moran gets back to me: Chaminade has their own playoff game on Thursday, so they feel a Tuesday scrimmage with us doesn't give them any time to recover.

May 16

At practice we begin installation of the famous Melville "Backer D," just in case. We have played tough man-to-man all year, with a few different slide packages, but people basically know what we do. The "Backer" package is a little something extra for West Islip and beyond, if we are so fortunate. It may catch them by surprise. It may force a single turnover. And a single turnover could make the difference, we are so close in ability. After practice we have a coach's meeting to decide post-season awards. There are tough choices to make this year. Our squad has good balance, and almost everybody has had a good year.

May 17

We announce that Andrew Maurer made All-American, the 51s^t out of Ward Melville. Giardinello was named Honorable mention All-American. Mazzone, Ward, DeVore, Alex Blechman, and Pennington made All-County. Kelaher earned All-Division. We have so many good kids, if you were a starter for us this year, you were All-County caliber, is the way I look at it. Kresse and Westermann shutout almost everybody they covered and got zero recognition. Ben-Eliyahu was the second-leading scorer on the third-ranked team in the country and deserved something, but it becomes a numbers game when every team in the Division has to be represented.

The weather is getting hot and the boys complained they were thirsty toward the end of practice. I sat them down in a pile of dirt and told them what a 110 degree day in Baghdad might be like with an M-16 rifle and a ninety-pound knapsack.

They stopped their whining immediately.

May 19

I can't sleep at night. I am worried sick about this Sachem East playoff game. We haven't played a tough game in so long, I don't know what we'll look like if we're challenged. I know we have the better players, but that doesn't always win it. They have the single best player in the country in Perritt, and who knows what could happen. We could lay an egg and be finished.

We celebrate our 24 seniors and their parents on the field at Guam before the game. The Moms gets hugs and flowers, the Dads get hugs and Ward Melville lacrosse hats. Every boy has his moment in the spotlight. While I'm shaking their hands my stomach is in a double-knot. But I need not have worried. Perritt shows up in street clothes and Coach Mercurio tells me he was injured in their last game and can't go at all today.

Ben-Eliyahu got us rolling right away with a sweet feed to Ward. Bang! 1-0 Patriots. Kresse stripped his man of the ball and found Giardinello, who passed to Ben-Eliyahu, Bang! 2-0. Ward found Kunkel alone. Bang! It's 3-0 at end of the first quarter, each goal the result of a good pass. That's what this team does, find each other, and why they are so hard to contain. They move the rock, and don't care who shoots.

Alex Blechman scored a man-up goal to open the second quarter. Giardinello faked out everybody and pounded home a jump-shot. Ward fed Giardinello. Giardinello fed Mazzone (who also picked up a 11 ground balls in the game). Kelaher fired the first of his three goals past the now-mesmerized goalie. We lead 9-2 at the half and put it on cruise-control.

In the second half, in front of back-up goalies Josh Blechman and AJ Heeren, Maurer, DeVore, Kresse, Rahner, Micele, Redko and long-stick midfielders Routi and Westermann held the frustrated visitors scoreless. Blaney continued his face-off dominance and scored a goal. Jared Blechman got one. Brous got two goals and almost got three. Nagle could have had scored a second goal, but he ran past their goalie and held his fire as time expired.

On the defensive end Maurer started a fast break off his knees and de-sticked a kid with a check. (Our boys yell "Yahtzzee!" when a check knocks the opponent's stick free) Kresse absolutely destroyed two kids who tried to "take" him to the cage. I'm amazed that people don't realize how good Matt is getting. He should be hearing from Virginia and Syracuse by now, Top Five places like that.

In the locker room we learned that William Floyd beat Half Hollow Hill East, so we are back to where we started our season for our semifinal match-up: facing Andrew Miller, who had six goals and an assist in his team's 14-7 win. Northport and West Islip advanced and will play each other Tuesday in the second game. Like I told Kaspar: I'm rooting for his Northport Tigers to beat West Islip. Kaspar promises me they can whip them and us. I just laugh.

I've known Kapsar for a million years, and been his business partner since the early 1990's when we merged my Suffolk Lacrosse Camp with his Four-Star Lacrosse Camp. I started my camp in 1969 at the Lake Grove School with Three Village children. I did it so we could get better, and bond as a team. But when Jim suggested a merger I was only too happy to join forces. By then I was tired of the summer camp business, and sensitive to some irresponsible behavior by my former players/counselors. For three years we ran the camp out at Southampton College. For three years I kept catching my counselors in Hampton nightclubs rather than back in the dorms where they were supposed to be, supervising their young charges. Then they couldn't get up to referee the morning sessions, so I would have to do it myself. I decided I didn't want a lawsuit with my name on it, and I didn't want to have to be a disciplinarian to them in the summer, too. Let big Jim yell at everybody. That's what he's good at.

Kaspar was an assistant coach at Nassau Community College for 17 of their glory years. He was for six years the head coach at McArthur High in Levittown. He was head coach at Baldwin High for a dozen years. He was my assistant for a year at Ward Melville, and has now spent three years at Northport. He knows the game inside and out, and honestly thinks, if they get by West Islip, they can beat us. But I don't think we'll see them. West Islip is too fast and tough, too blue-collar. They'll guard the crap out of those Northport All-Americans.

Me, I hope nobody on our team does anything dumb tonight. I feel like the worried parent of forty wayward sons.

May 22

On the NCAA Championship weekend we hold an early practice on Sunday to keep them on their toes. I tend to focus on the task at hand at this time of the year. Playoff time is payoff time. The pressure and intensity increases as we move through the brackets. Our game last Friday was difficult for me because of my friendship with Rick Mercurio, the Sachem East coach. I wanted our guys to play well and win convincingly, but at the same time not wanting to embarrass Sachem East. I was proud of our guys. They were gentlemen, displaying good sportsmanship. Nagle had that chance to score a garbage goal as time ran out and he held his fire. Rick appreciated that gesture, and said as much to the Newsday reporter. With Sachem and Ward Melville there is always mutual respect between the players. These guys have battled each other hundreds of times since grade school.

We had a good practice in the rain this morning, and worked hard on preparing for William Floyd. They're a solid team, not a great team. We beat them handily the first game of the season without Giardinello. Hopefully this game will go the same way. We know what we have to do—stop Andrew Miller and continue to play good team defense.

May 24

The county semifinals double-header is where our last four seasons have unhappily ended, and we don't want that to happen again. We've come too far and worked too hard. The forecast is for high winds and heavy rain. If we win, we may not stick around to watch the second game as we usually do. I don't want anyone sick. After dropping their season opener to us, the Colonials (13-4) enjoyed a terrific season.

The game was played at Comsewogue. Fortunately, Ben-Eliyahu doesn't mind rotten conditions. Or he doesn't complain. He's the second leading scorer on the nation's third-ranked team and he was overlooked for post-season recognition. Not a peep out of Jason. On Tuesday, when we were misfiring and needed him most, Jason delivered a five-goal performance. Joining Ben-Eliyahu in the scoring column for us were Giardinello and Kunkel with two goals apiece. Jared Blechman and Kelaher each scored once. Another senior who made sure we advanced to our first County Final since 2000 was Nick Ward (Maryland), who passed out five assists. Maurer played a great game again on defense as Floyd kept coming at us. I'm glad we held on. The Colonials improved quite a lot this year.

May 25

We're back in the big games now and it just feels right. Newsday cares what I think again and television cameras abound. Barry Landers and Art Kaminsky interview me before the game, and I can see that we have won some respect back this season. I hear the old buzz-words: "Undefeated and Powerhouse Program." I hear Cuozzo has "quieted his critics." They rave about my awesome defense and All-County goalie, our solid middies, Joey and Benny on fire at attack. You have to know that this is great fun for a guy who is basically a high school physical education teacher. This is the biggest dance we've got.

#

We have more atrocious weather today, worse than yesterday. Cold rain and high winds hammer Long Island. If I were in charge of Section 8, I'd move the Nassau championship games at Hofstra University to tomorrow afternoon and evening.

I'll be watching the West Islip-Northport (17-12) game re-played on television tonight, see one more time how they both scored all those goals. I don't think we'll score 12 on them tomorrow, but I know they won't score 17 on us. Who will step up and be great for us?

Better be everybody.

May 26

Massapequa won the Nassau Class A championship game over Hicksville easily last night at Hofstra in lousy weather. Hewlett beat Garden City. Manhasset beat archrival Cold Spring Harbor. Only Hewlett winning is a surprise to me, but they have the big kid Max Siebald who is headed to Cornell. I'll think about Massapequa later. They have an inspirational story going on down there with Hopkins-bound Mike Powers battling cancer, but so do we. They have good kids on that team, but so do we.

We arrange to practice at LaValle and consider the variety of different looks on defense we can show them. Heck, maybe we'll just lockout their three attackmen and let our middies play their middies for the title. A possibility I consider.

No classes are scheduled for tomorrow, but we'll have a quick walk-through and a team lunch catered by the parents at school to keep the boys occupied. Eight at night is a long time to wait to play a game. I'll be a wreck from the moment I wake up.

May 27

I watched Mount Sinai coached by Mike Hoppey lose in overtime to Tom Rotanz and his Shoreham Wading River Wildcats. Both head coaches played at Ward Melville for me. I sit off to the side and watch quietly, not rooting for anyone. Then I drive back to our school to get ready to get on the bus. I hate the night game. I'm always ready to play at noon. We could draw five thousand fans tonight, the Section XI rep tells me. Everybody wants this re-match.

But during the Huntington-Sayville game a small storm rolls past and the game is called off for lightning. Then our game is cancelled due to lightning that won't ever happen. Two hours later the field is dry and the skies are filled with stars.

Nobody had a television or a cell phone? We couldn't learn that this was a rogue cell and would leave the area in thirty minutes? Our team school bus got in a fender-bender accident on the way back to Ward Melville, then somebody said something disrespectful and dumb to the cops taking the accident report. Bill Martens and I yelled at them to show some damn class, which put the kids in a foul mood, which only made the coaches' foul mood worse. We got back to school, but nobody asked the question: "Who bad?"

We were so ready to play that night. Maybe they were, too.

May 28

We hold a light practice, and we try to put the good morale back on track. But something is missing, some of the swagger and some of the undefeated love for each other.

May 29

On a glorious day for lacrosse we came out strong, winning the first few groundball battles and setting up our offense, which averaged over twelve goals a game in 2005. Ward found Kunkel to give us a quick one-goal lead. West Islip's Gary Messina (Quinnipiac) dodged from the top to tie it at one. Alex Blechman scored one for us on his favorite play, a hard sweep right and a top-shelf rocket.

West Islip—who averaged fifteen goals a game this year—answered with a pair of second quarter goals, one by a Lion defenseman on a clear, to take a three-to-two lead at the half. A short third-period pass from All-American Matt Sullivan to All-County Kevin Federico set up the fourth West Islip goal.

The final quarter began with our crowd pleading for a comeback, something we have engineered this year from deeper holes than this. Giardinello gave them hope with an unassisted goal to pull us within one with nine minutes left. But only thirty seconds later the Lion's burly creaseman Ryan Euell buried a pass from Matt Sullivan to extend the lead to two, a crippling blow from which we would not recover. West Islip scored one more mop-up goal as we gambled and hustled until the clock ran out. The loss is devastating, and I know immediately this year will not satisfy some of our more critical fans and former players.

We finished 18-1, with the Division I Championship, the #5 spot in the national polls, and the #1 Academic ranking of any public school lacrosse team in New York State. Still, people will bash me and the other coaches for failing to advance to the Long Island championship game and beyond. Right now, I don't care. I'm so frustrated I could scream. We scored three goals in a county final. You can't win like that. Not against a team this good. We had the lead early, and then made a bad mistake allowing Christian Scuderi's goal. I don't think Ward took him seriously in time, until all he had available was a one-handed wrap-check that Scuderi ran through. On the very next face-off, Westermann went over-the-head on Pete Mezzanotte (Towson) for a strip, but the ball bounced back to Mezzanotte and he took off down the field. Westermann chased him, hacking away, but Mezzanotte is a track star and Westermann couldn't close the gap, which surprised DeVore, who thought he wouldn't need to slide. Mezzanotte, on the gallop, bounced one into the upper corner on Pennington, who looked equally surprised.

During our second-half comeback, we cut the margin to 4-3, but Maurer got caught ball-watching by Matt Sullivan, and Federico found him alone. Bang—that was all it took, just a couple of mistakes, or a couple of great plays by the Lions. It depends on how you look at it.

But mainly we couldn't score. We didn't answer back. Every Patriot dodge was blocked, every cut covered. Their junior goalie Sal Barcia (Robert Morris) made a few great saves for them and we took a few bad shots, but it was hard to get any shots off at all in the second half, their defense played so well.

The locker room back at Melville was cemetery quiet, devastated. Nobody asked: "Who bad?" when we got to the high school driveway. There were sniffles as they turned in their equipment. Just before I left the building, I looked in the locker room and saw Westermann, who will be back next year, head down in a towel, sitting in his shredded underwear next to our boy who is sick, and who knows he has played his last lacrosse game.

May 31

At the Spring Sports Awards Night I announce my retirement from teaching physical education, but state my intention to continue coaching the team. We are honored for winning the Division I title, our first since 2000, and our 18-0 record before losing in the County Final. Unsung Hero awards go to Ben-Eliyahu, Smith, Blaney, and Kresse. The 2005 Patriots win the #1 academic ranking among boys' lacrosse teams in New York State—the team with the best grade-point-average. Our guys were truly scholars and athletes and gentlemen in 2005. They carried the load well, and made us proud of the team all year long. They lost only one game of nineteen. But it was a big game.

June 11

We finish our year with our Alumni game. Bob Betcher (Ohio Wesleyan) and Chris Walker (UNC) helps to organize the event and all his brothers play in it. Their father Bob Walker is the volunteer scorekeeper, and their children arrive for the game in hand-me down Patriot-wear. The head of the vast Nagle clan usually refs the game. And this year—as if they spent the last few weeks in their back yard practicing together again—the Nagle boys provided the scoring for the victorious Gelinas squad. Six goals and a Nagle in on every one of them, several of them Mike Nagle-to-Mark Nagle give-and-goes. George Gleusner was spectacular in the cage for the winners. He gave up an underhand rocket to Kevin Morris (Oklahoma State wrestler) in the first half and only one more goal the rest of the way—to Bob MacDevitt ('71), who has now scored a goal in eight straight Alumni games. Also on the field with plenty in the tank were John Fox (UNC), Tom Brown (UMass), John and Rich Wilkens of Johns Hopkins, and big George Schmidt, who can still stop a fast break cold. Former NCAA Player of the Year Dennis Goldstein (UNC) was on hand, with his dad in tow. Shoreham-Wading River Head Coach Tom Rotanz played defense at Ward Melville, and now runs one of the top-flight high school programs on the Island. Charlie Brown (Washington and Lee) a star from the 70's, was an All-American goalie, but he chose to run midfield, where he "could make a mistake and not everybody knows about it." This year's game raised funds to buy the current varsity new uniforms.

The fun began on Friday night with a chalk talk at Mario's Restaurant. We played the game on Saturday afternoon. Betch always runs a raffle to benefit the program, then the players limp home and ice-up. Saturday night the brotherhood reconvenes for dinner and cocktails and war stories. The older they get, the better they were. But these guys don't need to exaggerate. Some of those former boys running around on Saturday never lost a high school lacrosse game.

Andrew Maurer (44) squares off with Pat Perritt (1) for a groundball.

Nick Ward (22) fires at the top shelf.

Photos by: Bruce Larrabee

Nick Tsouris (1) surrounded by West Islip Lions.

Ken Mazzone (16) finishes a Jason Ben-Eliyahu (32) assist.

Photos by: Bruce Larrabee

Joey Giardinello (33) buries a jump-shot while
Alex Blechman (9) looks on.

Matt Kresse (40) starts a fast break

Photos by: Bruce Larrabee

Steven Rastivo (2) stones Lion star Kevin Federico (3).

Jake Westermann (35) covers Kevin Federico while
Steven Rastivo (2) looks on.

Photos by: Bruce Larrabee

2006 Preseason

The first I heard that something was up with the varsity lacrosse coaching position at Ward Melville was when I was playing golf with our athletic director, Don Webster. As I was addressing my ball on the first tee at Fox Hill Country Club, Don said to me, "Joe, it doesn't look good for you coaching this spring."

I stepped back, looked at him, and said, "What do you mean it doesn't look good?" I mean, I've only held the job for 37 years.

Webster said that Mike Hoppey, a former player and assistant of mine, had applied for the position after I retired from teaching, and the teachers' union was supporting him since he was a full-time employee in the building and I wasn't. Needless to say I was surprised by the news. I had always been led to believe I would be allowed to continue coaching lacrosse after retiring from full-time teaching. Others saw this as an opening and seized the opportunity. I had hoped to coach the boys for another few years, and I felt I had earned the right to choose my own departure. The situation I expected would not have been unprecedented. It is how things are done at Farmingdale High School, among others. There was a minor uproar in the lacrosse community, and some newspaper and magazine articles and letters to the editor, and a few hard feelings, including my own. I'll leave it to others to decide if this was the proper way to terminate my career as head coach at Ward Melville. But I never thought so.

Ultimately, Hoppey and I got together and decided that the best thing for the team was to make 2006 a transition year. We would serve as co-head coaches for the year, and then Mike will take over alone for the 2007 season. I'm not sure what I'll do after that, or where I'll go, but I plan to stay in game at some level.

#

Our returning players enjoyed their experience in the Three Village evening summer league at Stony Brook University again, on the turf in the stadium against Northport, Smithtown, Sachem, Rocky Point and other good schools. They attended the Four-Star Challenge Camp at UMass as a team. Then they broke up and went to various recruiting camps, including Top 205 at Maryland, the Brown Camp for those interested in New England colleges, and Hotbeds at University of Delaware for those boys who had not yet firmed up a college situation by the end of the summer. Kresse played with DeVore on the LI Empire team and committed to UMBC. Tsouris and Kelaher made the Top 205 All-Star team and landed deals with Yale and Delaware. Long-stick middie Jon Ferro fulfilled his dream and committed to Virginia Military Institute. Nagle and Redko won over the Ursinus coaches. Connor McCabe committed to Roger Williams College. Droesch nailed down his dream-school, Tufts. Droesch is an All-State swimmer who also scored 2190 on the new SAT, our new team record. Seventeen of our 2006 boys will play lacrosse next year in college, eight in Division 1.

I like the team-summer-camp concept for bonding next year's players, for holding unofficial tryouts, and the good experience of newcomers playing the game at the faster speed. I still think the best way for a college coach to judge a high school player is with his own team in a game that matters. But that's just me and I'm old school. I realize not every good player gets to play in games that matter. Hence the rise of club teams and travel teams that cost lots of money and time. Parents want to see their boys recruited to better colleges than their grades alone would attract. But it's not as easy as it looks. I hear a lot about club teams from Long Island that drove four hours to play another team from Long Island for a tournament championship we could have settled behind Murphy Junior High in South Setauket or on Buffalo Avenue in Freeport.

We told the skinny ones to lift weights in the off-season, the chubby ones to run a lot and work on their speed. Everybody does their wall-ball and stick work, or they better. At a summer league game with Northport we say farewell to Kaspar, who leaves the Tiger sideline to take the head-coaching job at Long Beach. Our boys thank him for everything he's done for them. He's a gruff old bastard, but the kids know he's on their side when they need him.

Coach Hoppey and his assistant Bryan Miller—a defenseman for me in the Eighties who came over with Mike from Mt. Sinai—ran a team in the Fall-Ball League at Farmingdale State on Sunday mornings for the boys who didn't play a fall sport. The competition is decent, not great, without the football and soccer players. It's a chance to play, and a chance for coaches to evaluate incoming talent. Until March, the rest of our preseason work will take place at the indoor facility in Ronkonkoma, in the weight room, and the Ward Melville gym.

We have four returning starters who are top 20 Division I recruits and a solid senior class to back them. We will have difficulty replacing the all-around leadership and good play of Mazzone, the athleticism and aggression of Giardinello, the soft hands and toughness of Ben-Eliyahu, also the shooting of Nick Ward and Alex Blechman. Most of our rising junior middies have a ways to go before they're ready for the speed and ferocity of varsity play, but we do have a couple of promising sophomores in goalie Steve Rastivo (Penn State), attacker Zach Pall (Quinnipiac), middie Josh LaMantia (Drexel) and defensemen Matt Spagnoli (Bucknell). I am amazed sometimes at the way the good players just keep coming, year after year, class after class.

During the off-season I attended conventions, as you can always learn something. At the US Lacrosse meeting in Baltimore I see college coaches who want to talk about my boys, whom should they go after. People who have studied our methods tell me, "Hey, Joe, at my high school in Massachusetts we're playing the Backer D."

I gave the keynote speech in Atlanta, and got a plaque from someone every time I turned around. And everywhere I went I heard, what the hell's happening at Ward Melville? How could they do that to you? I tell them life is full of surprises, and we're going to make one last run for the roses as a team. Then I don't know.

I'd like to say goodbye to my upstate rival Mike Messere of West Genny on the field at LaValle—right after we've won the State title. That may be asking a lot of this team, but that's something else we do at Ward Melville. We ask a lot, because they get so much back. Also, this year I will do my utmost to keep in mind what a friend said, one of the Drivers Ed teachers. He told me during this final season to take everything in, the smell of grass and the sounds of the locker room, the laughter of the boys, the excitement and adrenaline, and the tears. Don't let it race by you, he said. Easier said than done.

Something else changed in my life during the off-season. In December of 2005 I went with some teachers to watch Mike Carubia, a jazz musician and former Ward Melville music teacher, perform with his swing band at Five Towns College. After the show we went for pizza with some of the musicians and their friends. I sat at a long table next to a pretty woman I didn't know. She asked me what I did, so I told her. She asked what I did for fun besides lacrosse, and I mentioned skiing at Okemo Mountain in Ludlow, Vermont. She said she went there a lot with her sister. I asked where she lived. She told me her sister lived in Connecticut. I told her my brother lived there. She asked me what town. I told her Ridgefield. She looked at me funny, and asked what street. I told her Bennett's Farm Road. Her jaw dropped. "That's where my sister lives," she said. So our brothers and sisters are neighbors. At that point I was glad to find we two Italian-American school teachers weren't somehow related, because we've been dating ever since, and I'm as happy as I have been in years. Dave McCulloch (Hofstra), one of our all-time greats, called my cell the other day and asked me where I was. I had to confess to standing in the lingerie section of Bloomingdales. He whooped with laughter, and I didn't mind at all.

January 15

We got some bad news from the Peddie School Tournament, an indoor short-stick tournament in New Jersey. We sent a team coached by Dr. Jim Droesch down to the prep school, minus long-poles DeVore, Kresse, Westermann and Colin Field, and wrestlers like Belvedere, Chris Day (Army), and Spagnoli. We lost in the quarters or semis, I really don't care, but the bad news is our senior goalie John Matzelle broke his hand in warm-ups. Now we've gone from five good, healthy goalies last year, where it was hard to choose the starter, down to one or two. And probably the best healthy goalie is a sophomore with a big reputation but little experience. Good thing we have a defense coming back. Now, please—no more injuries, no more sick boys or dying relatives, no more heartbreak. Westermann's uncle with that fishing team in North Carolina passed away this winter, no matter how many times Jake wore the lucky T-shirt under his jersey on game days, no matter how hard he prayed to extend his life.

"Wear it again this year," I told him when he told me what happened.

"Thank you, coach. I'm going to."

Westermann told me that Mezzanotte's goal in the county final haunted him all year, that we had to get back to the finals and win it. I wasn't surprised. We re-live those big games again and again, the good and the bad. I think it will make him better. I told him that last year he was a good player, this year I expected him to be great. No excuses. He nodded, serious as hell. Some kids are so easy to coach. But I can already see that this is going to be an adjustment for me, sharing the responsibility and the leadership. I think the boys might need me to be more of a teammate this year and less of a coach.

#

From Don Webster, WM AD:

"Ward Melville High School is pleased to announce that Mike Hoppey has been appointed Boys Head Lacrosse Coach for the spring 2006 season. Longtime head coach Joe Cuozzo will serve as Associate Head Coach this spring and assist in bringing a smooth transition to the very successful program. Joe has served the district for the past 37 years, winning 31 League, 22 County, 15 LI, 9 Regional and 7 New York State Championships.

Mike is welcomed back to the Ward Melville High School lacrosse coaching ranks after serving as head coach at Mt. Sinai High School the past two years and taking his team to the Suffolk County Championship game both years. Mike is a 1974 graduate of Ward Melville where he garnered All-County honors in his senior season. He moved on to Cortland State, winning MVP and All-American honors in both 1977 and 1978. Mike was inducted into the Long Island Metropolitan Hall of Fame in 2000.

The combination of Mike and Joe will provide our student-athletes with the opportunity to be coached by two of the best coaches to come through Suffolk County and Long Island. Together their expertise will continue to have Ward Melville lacrosse in the upper echelon of programs in the state."

Blah, blah, blah, yada, yada, yada. They shouldn't have done it, especially after the year we had in 2005. No one has ever stepped forward to say who made the final decision to put me out. They can hide behind the union, but I don't buy it. Other places make exceptions to keep highly qualified educators around. No one ever had the guts to stand up to me and tell me why I had to go. They didn't show me any respect even though our school is known around the world because of our lacrosse program. People in Australia have heard of us. Nevertheless, I am finally a senior at Ward Melville, Class of 2006, after 37 years as a perpetual junior, after making the National Hall of Fame. For the first time ever, as my guys leave here, I will go with them. It is a bitter pill.

March 6

It's hard to believe the 2006 season is already here. Seems like yesterday we walked off the field at Stony Brook, heartbroken. I have decided my personal goal for this last year is to work my ass off for the guys, and to have fun myself. I want this year to be the most enjoyable of my career. I am excited to be working again with seniors DeVore, Kresse and Westermann—though we will miss our great All-American Andrew Maurer. These three players will again form the nucleus of the most imposing defensive unit on Long Island, if not in the country. We have a solid senior goalie in Jon Matzelle who has never lost a junior varsity or junior high game. Matzelle's broken thumb is healthy for opening day. But he's so tough, he wouldn't let me know if his leg was hanging off. Behind him we have perhaps the best sophomore in the country in Steve Rastivo (Penn State.) I'm not just saying that because he's mine. I've seen some good goalies here, like the aforementioned Greg Cattrano. On his work ethic alone, Rastivo will be great. The national scouts have Rastivo rated top-shelf along with Tyler Fiorito of McDonogh and Steven Burke at Bullis. Rastivo's spent his childhood working out under the guidance of Cattrano and Nick Gentilesco, another of our guys that played for Brown. Every college coach in the country will be after Steve-o because his grades are good, too.

Kelaher returns to face-off and run first midfield. He will be joined by Droesch and Tsouris. Greg Sefarian (Boston College) has fought his way back after an ACL injury he suffered wrestling, and could be a face-off specialist. Dominick Belvedere (Duke-wrestling) is a defensive middie and an All-County safety on the football team. Kunkel, now a junior, with his great stick skills, and lefty Duggan (Siena) both saw time at attack last year. Beltrani (Marist) and Nagle (Ursinus) should contribute right away. After that, who knows? We need a few long-poles to step up to give us depth, a few more middies that can play both ends. But basically the team has returned in good shape, without any holdover injuries.

Coach Hoppey and I asked them to get stronger and faster and better during the off-season and most of them have improved. It's been cold on Long Island, with last week's snow slowly disappearing. We'll work in the gym today and hope we get to 40 degrees tomorrow.

March 7

These first few days are filled with mixed emotions for me, excited to be on the field with the guys again, at the same time feeling poignant that this is my last first week at Ward Melville. This co-coach situation is going to take some getting use to—not as easy as I thought it would be. I start to say things to the guys and then shut up, not wanting to step on toes. What is my place? What is not my place? I don't know. We'll work it out, I hope. People at Ward Melville seem to relate to me in a different way, almost as if I'm an honored visitor now, or have need to be pitied. I don't want honors or pity or to make people uncomfortable, so now I always go in the back door of the high school and stay out of the hallways. I feel less a part of the whole thing.

#

We are once again more blue-collar than white, the kids of plumbers and uniformed services. (Rastivo's dad Russ is a Suffolk County corrections officer. Kresse is the son of a New York City fireman. Westermann's dad is an ex-cop. Kelaher is the son of a Suffolk detective and a school teacher.

As I study the projected starters, I realize every one of them lives in an intact household with his own two biological parents—except Westermann lives with his dad and stepmother. You don't see stability like that very often these days, even in an affluent district like ours.

At my end of the field I'm feeling pretty good about my gang of long-poles and goalies. There seems to be a strong bond between us all left over from the last few years. Redko and Matt Godsell (USMMA) will battle for playing time with Colin Field (Cortland), a junior basketball player, and Matt Spagnoli, a sophomore who wrestles and plays football. Tom O'Connor (Georgetown) is again on the bubble to make the team, trying his butt off, as usual. Matzelle (CW Post) had a great practice today, stopping everything, trying to hold off the sophomore phenom. Rastivo looked a little nervous in the cage, and I don't blame him. These big guys shoot hard. I'll bet Kelaher and Kunkel hit ninety-miles-an-hour if they get their feet set. That takes some getting used to. All of this will take some getting used to. But keep your eye on Rastivo. He has the makings of a great one.

March 14

We make the final cuts. This year the onus was mostly on Coach Hoppey, and I was glad to let him shoulder that burden. We sent some good boys home, and I know they are devastated. A few juniors with potential to improve we ask to continue their development with the junior varsity. They are good enough to make the team, and we want to keep them playing, but we just don't have room at their positions on the varsity. This is a real challenge to their core identities, and we give them a few days to think it over. Fortunately, Tom O'Connor, who took that tough road last year, made the varsity with hustle and attitude and grit, and if there was a happier boy at practice this afternoon, I didn't see him. Even if Tom doesn't get to play in games that much, I think it sends a good signal that hard work and loyalty is rewarded. Not everybody is born with the ability to run a 4.8 forty-yard dash. But everybody can get better through hard work. Let' see if any of those sent-down juniors this year get the message. I heard from the other guys that Tommy's college application essay to Georgetown (he got in!) was about the humbling experience of playing JV as a junior, the only kid with a certain color helmet. I guess we teach our boys all kinds of lessons here.

March 15

On the Ides of March, we have wind and cold on the field turf at Comsewogue. We were pleased with our individual and team defense in the scrimmage. Middies did a nice job against their good young players like Al Kohart (Penn) and John DiChiaro (Dartmouth). Unfortunately our attack was a disaster, especially in transition. Our defense started four clean fast breaks and we scored no goals. We are sadly lacking in a quarterback, someone who can create and make things happen, a slashing dodger-feeder like Giardinello. Beltrani and Duggan are such laid-back guys. Both need to play with more passion. They need to take over that end. And Kunkel looks like a fish out of water trying to dodge with the ball. He belongs out on the wing, sneaking into space to fire his rocket. Right now Coach Hoppey has Kunkel playing behind the net in the 2-2-2 set. We both are kind of shocked at the situation. Mike and I both thought this unit would gel quickly. It's not my bailiwick this season, so I don't say much. But we need to work out this attack if we want to go anywhere this year.

The challenge is considerable. Last year we won eighteen games before losing to West Islip in the finals. We were ranked as high as third in the nation before slipping to #14. Inside Lacrosse Magazine has given us a preseason national ranking of #16. West Islip is ranked 4th, Northport 14th. New York State Class A Champion West Genesee is ranked first. Again this year I will concentrate on the defensive end of the field. Also joining the Patriot staff this year is John Delucia, a superb midfielder from our 1997 State Championship team.

2006 Regular Season

March 18

We scrimmage Huntington, a veteran State Championship team that's ranked fifth in the country, with one of the top recruits for this year and three for next year. On a cold and windy day at Huntington we get off to a good start, playing them straight up, get a 1-0 lead, and hold it for ten minutes. Then they rocked us for a few.

We made adjustments and got some great individual match-ups: Sammy DeVore against Zach Howell (Duke). Westermann slid out to play LSM against Scott Kocis (Georgetown). Kresse against Austin Carino. The Bratton (Virginia) twins against Tsouris—who can run with them—and Kelaher, who almost can. But their coaches are smart guys, too, and this is just what they wanted to practice against a good team. After a while they identified our slower middies and beat them like dogs. Speed kills in lacrosse.

And again our attack was terrible, unable to maintain possession so our poles could catch a breath. We committed dumb penalties, and lots of careless turnovers and lost 10-4. This was a good wake-up call for us. Sometimes our kids think they can just toss their jocks out on the field and the other guys will fold. Not the Huntington Blue Devils. Those guys are seriously good and I can see them winning everything again.

Driving back to Setauket, I recall we've played against a lot of great players over the years. Roy Colsey of Yorktown and Syracuse, now the MLL. Doug Shanahan of Sachem/Hofstra/MLL. The Nelson brothers and the Marrs from Yorktown. Billy Dwan from Yorktown, now a coach at Johns Hopkins. AJ Haugen of Bethpage and Princeton and the MLL. Corey Harned played attack at Sachem and made All-American as an LSM at Johns Hopkins. The Pettit brothers from Huntington and West Point were incredible young men. Drew Thompson (Virginia) and Kyle Dowd (Duke) from Northport. Ray Enners (Army), God rest his soul, from Half Hollow Hills. Matt Danowski

(Duke) and Steve Panarelli (Syracuse) from Farmingdale. Matt Zash from Duke and Massapequa. Good opponents teach us to get better, so we put them on our schedule all we can. I figure we learned some lessons at Huntington, humility being one of them. But we found our goalie in the second half, the aforementioned Rastivo. We also found our long-pole middie in Colin Field, and maybe another potential attackman in sophomore Zach Pall. We're still shopping for a couple middies and some backup defensemen for the man-down team and to spell Field at pole now and then. The sophomore Spagnoli has separated himself from the pack of defensemen. We think he's going to be a good one. Godsell and Redko do a nice job on our man-down team.

Also at Huntington I was disappointed by the lack of composure from some of our "veterans." We need to play confidant, disciplined lacrosse if we want to be successful. One-on-one-displays of physical dominance look dumb when they draw a flag, and are followed by an easy Huntington goal. Coach Hoppey told our guys he was disappointed but not discouraged, and I think that's right. We need to adjust our line-up to get as much offense as possible out on the field. We need Duggan to get his ankle healthy and dominate. We have a long way to go.

March 19

The lax parents met at the Kelaher's house, where the veterans indoctrinated the newbies. They told them how important grades are when thinking of colleges, what to expect in the recruiting process, the best summer camps if you son is not plucked early. The team-parents chip in to pay for our advance scouting films. They schedule the pasta parties, one of the most popular parts of playing Patriot lax. They remind each other this will all be over in the blink of an eye, to enjoy it while they may, kind of a theme for all of us here this year. And one of our junior middies lets us know he will play a second season of junior varsity ball to earn a chance to make the varsity next year. Tom O'Connor has indeed been a good example.

March 20

To shake things up, Coach Hoppey has sophomore Zach Pall move to the starting attack, and seniors Beltrani and Nagle slide to the second midfield. I actually like the look of this arrangement, keeping more good shooters on the field. Now they need to play together and develop some familiarity. They also need to ride hard and get ground balls. So we'll see.

A work-in-progress. The junior class is not much help this year, providing only two starters.

March 21

The boys voted for captains and selected Kelaher, Kresse and DeVore. We are working more in units now to prepare for Chaminade—another good test for us. My defense works on slide-packages (from crease, from adjacent, no-slide) and the various man-down situations. We work on giving Rastivo the confidence to direct the defense, to tell the seniors where to go and when. Through the grapevine we learn that our rivals in the A Division are struggling right now, too. West Islip, like us, is still holding tryouts. Scott Craig has three-quarters of his team set, and those guys are good. Attackman Kevin Federico is headed to UNC, Pete Mezzanotte is going to Towson and Christian Scuderi is headed to NYIT and then Hofstra. Bob Macaluso's Northport team can't play defense well enough to beat us, at least not yet. An excellent kid named Mike Mizvesky headed to Navy, returns on defense. But everybody else is a converted basketball player or an untried underclassman. Scott Dale, an All-County goalie from Sachem North, and his family have moved there and he could be a big help. The Northport offense? The Empire team, basically, the gold standard. Craig Dowd (Gerogetown), Max Bartig (Syracuse), Max Chautin (Hopkins), Travis Burr (Harvard), Max Mancuso (Washington & Lee) and Tom Lucky (Colgate). Burr and Bartig went to the county finals in the basketball playoffs on smarts and athleticism, so they might be a bit behind in their stick-work. The Tigers will miss my buddy Jimmy Kasper, too. Jim has one of the great minds in the high school game and is always a barrel of fun. The Northport kids will miss him.

Smithtown West has a veteran team with a great young attack of Scott Perri (Drexel) and Rob Pannell (Cornell) and a rookie head coach, Greg Foster, an assistant to Kevin Huff for the last five years. They are good, deep, smart, and I worry about them. If we have the best defense in Suffolk, West Islip's and theirs with Matt Stefurak (Delaware), Brennan Bailey (Brown) and Mike Eng are second and third. And their goalies Joe Marra (Fairfield) and Brian Pilnacek (Quinnipiac) are also excellent. Middie Brian Smalley (Loyola) is a dangerous lefty. The talent in Suffolk is spreading wider and deeper. The two Sachems have some young guns and will fight us with every fiber of their being. But the district split really hurt them last year. May it be the same for them again.

March 22

The latest edition of Inside Lacrosse Magazine is on newsstands and Sam DeVore has been named the national pre-season Defenseman of The Year. In the Top 25 Team round-up were are picked right behind Northport. Duggan, Kunkel, Tsouris, Droesch, Kelaher, Kresse, Westermann, Matzelle and Rastivo all got ink, so we hang it on the locker room bulletin board. We play an intra-squad game to get ready to scrimmage Chaminade, who will get us ready to play Sayville on opening day.

Westermann, DeVore and Kresse have come to realize that I still live alone in my condo on the beach out east, and have taken to asking my plans at night, what I will have for dinner, will I be alone, like they need to take care of me like I'm some doddering old fool who doesn't eat right. I appreciate their concern, but then I ask them right back. Many nights they get home from lacrosse practice and eat meals thrown together by parents who work multiple jobs, night shifts. Me, I can cook for myself, thank you, but lately my meals are prepared by that certain young woman I met in December. Lucretia is a gourmet chef, and I eat quite well. I crack up when they say they're having Taco Bell and Gatorade, or something called a "Gasm" from the deli and a large iced-tea, while I'm having roast pork, new potatoes, spinach salad and nice white wine from a local vineyard.

March 23

I have always believed in scrimmaging good teams in order to evaluate our needs and weaknesses. Chaminade has an excellent coaching staff as well as the ability to attract good players from all over Nassau County. We don't have that luxury. Finding the right guys at Ward Melville is an ongoing process. Seniors are given first choice to prove themselves. If they don't measure up, we look at youngsters. Everyday is an evaluation day at practice. Most of the pieces are in place now except for one or two middies. We like the way the guys move the ball up and down the field. Now, if our attack could only finish by putting the ball in the damn net. A few of the seniors are unhappy as they see what is unfolding. It's up to them to work harder to get the job done, rather than blaming the coaches or sending their parents up to the school to plead their cases. It's an opportunity to take responsibility for themselves.

March 25

On the rear field at Ward Melville, the place affectionately known as Guam, we do a very nice job against (# 15 in the nation) Chaminade, coached by my buddy Jack Moran. They have 17 college recruits on this team. We start Steve Rastivo in goal and he plays well. DeVore and Westermann play tough defense against Gibson (Yale) and Colin Tighe (Providence), but Kresse tries to do too much against Chris Ahern (Lehigh) and Ahern, a clever stick-handler, makes him pay a few times. Beltrani plays well at attack, gets us a goal and an assist. Zach Pall scores again. Kelaher and Droesch and Nick Tsouris all play well at midfield. Pat Nagle, for his first time at his new position, looks good out there. Junior JC Ward, the third Ward brother to play here after Mike (Duke) and Nick (Maryland), scores on a bounce shot to put us ahead 5-4 at the end of the third period. Both squads pulled the starters then, happy to play a basically even match. It means we're ready to start our non-league schedule against Sayville, who was actually leading Huntington last year in the Final when lightning struck. Huntington came back on Sunday to win. But it was close. Sayville is an improving program among the Class B schools, a team stocked with a few good lacrosse players and a lot of football players. They will come after us on Monday like it's another Suffolk final. We tell our boys: They have nothing to lose, so be ready to match their physical intensity.

March 27

After a string of chilly afternoons, opening day was sunny and warm. A large crowd filled the bleachers and hugged the rail to watch. Sayville came hoping to set the Long Island lacrosse community abuzz with an early season upset. They left Guam hoping to rebound from a disappointing loss. Duggan scored a career-high five goals and dished one assist. Kunkel had a six-point game with three goals and three assists. Beltrani added a goal and an assist to Pat Nagle. JC Ward assisted on the Beltani goal. Young Pall scored his first varsity goal. Tsouris got our scoring started on a dodge from the top and a left-handed bounce-shot. Droesch did exactly the same thing to make it two-nothing. Kevin Kelaher bounced three bombs off the top pipe before finishing a nice assist from Beltrani.

We told our kids Sayville might be intimidated coming to play at Ward Melville for the first time ever. We told them to jump on them early, and the boys executed the plan. A six-one first quarter, and their only goal came in a man-down situation. DeVore even took it up the field and added an assist.

Division I play begins next week. I think we're ready. We are currently ranked 14th in the nation and 8th on Long Island. The victory over Sayville was number 684 for the program. We are back in season and I am fully alive.

March 29

In truth, Sayville bounced us around some, and we had 6 of our guys unable to practice yesterday because of injuries. We thought a day off would do them good since we have been going pretty hard since day one, refresh their legs, and give the injured a chance to heal. I'm a big believer in spending practice time on conditioning. It pays off mentally as well as physically. I tell them we will never lose a game because we are not in superb shape. This instills a feeling of confidence in the boys. I tell them the fourth quarter belongs to us. Teams may run with us for part of the game, but not for the full 48 minutes. They should be raring to go tomorrow.

We're going to be shorthanded on Saturday due to injuries and juniors at the SAT's. Don't know if we're going to see the real Ward Melville just yet. This will be a good opportunity for some of the other guys to step up. The junior middie we sent down to JV has fought his way back to the varsity already. What a smart move he made. Guts, and a love of the game are rewarded, sometimes quickly.

Sayville plays at West Islip this afternoon, so just that quickly I'm rooting for them, but it is probably a waste of time. West Islip will abuse them. Chaminade beat Massapequa 10-6 yesterday, maybe the best public school Class A team in Nassau. Based on how we've developed in our scrimmages, it looks like we might be in the mix again this year. And the weather is finally getting warmer. I peel off the first layer of the five layers of fleece I've been wearing.

March 30

West Islip 16, Sayville 3. About what I expected. Coach Craig knows what he's doing and they have a terrific feeder program. We are on different shores of this Island but very much alike as programs. Everyone in that uniform is a good lacrosse player, and some of them are great. Anyway, we got back to work with six players still unable to practice. The only one I'm really worried about is Kelaher's pulled quad. Those go on and on and on. Sixty-five degrees today, and the boys are feeling chipper.

April 1

At this year's Louis Acompora Scrimmages the local weatherman called for rain—but we got sunshine and warm steady breezes. In the early morning scrimmage we played Manhasset minus their seniors who had their Prom. But their youngsters were quite good, especially Petracca in goal and Connor English at attack, and they were fired up for us. We were sleepy and cocky and cranky and only won by one. Corning East is quick and lively and they wake us right up. We play a spirited 3-3 tie with them. Again our offense looks lousy but our defense does a good job chasing their quick little attack around the cage. The team from Wilton, Connecticut is going through a rebuilding year and just not at our level, and our third scrimmage features our youngsters running circles around them.

April 3

We start hounding our stars to play like stars. Time to step up and grow up. No more stupid penalties or dumb plays. We take the horrible rape accusations suddenly unfolding at Duke University and use it as a teaching opportunity on a variety of subjects—starting with drinking alcohol and moving on to how we treat women. Our boys listen hard because Mike Ward from Ward Melville is a star on that Duke team, an All-ACC middie whose stellar career and maybe more is suddenly in jeopardy. Thank God Mike was away from Durham that night for a job interview, so he can't be blamed for anything. I don't know what actually happened down there, and will wait to hear all the evidence before I form an opinion. Right now I just feel awful for Duke's head coach Mike Pressler, a very good friend of mine. This is every coach's nightmare.

April 4

We hold an easy practice today. The boys have been running hard and they need rest. They have their pasta party at the Godsell's house. Matt is 6'3", 190, a good football player and an excellent defenseman. He plays on the man-down team for us, and runs some long-pole. Next year Matt will play at the Merchant Marine Academy in Kings Point.

April 5

We win our Division opener over Longwood by a 16-4 margin. They lost their best player last week when a shot broke his jaw, and we peppered their plucky little goalie. Kunkel scored six goals on a variety of pretty shots. Duggan passed out six assists. Kelaher's quad is feeling better and he scored a pair. Tsouris had three assists, which is exactly what we're looking for from him on offense. He uses his speed to force a slide and makes a smart pass—boom, we get a goal. Junior attackman Ryan Molloy (Tufts) continues to impress the coaching staff and scored the first two goals of his varsity career. He's small but tough, a good student and hard worker. We were cutting to the crease and catching the ball and shooting and hitting the net, a thing of beauty. Had them down 15-1 at the end of three quarters when we pulled even our second lines.

Our reserves were a little out-gunned against the Longwood starters, and they allowed three fourth-quarter goals. I don't like how it pumps up our goals-allowed statistic, but it does serve to show those boys why they are not our starters. We'll hear no grumbling after the close games where they do not see the field. They'll be cheering for their teammates, relieved they are part of the event but not thrust into the spotlight where failure is always a misstep away. You get burned for a goal, and everybody in this town knows it, dissects what happened, worries that it might happen again.

At home that night I heard Mike Pressler had resigned the coaching job at Duke and the remainder of their 2006 season was cancelled. Wow. I've known Pressler for years, and love the guy. I can't imagine the heartbreak that he and his family are suffering. Talk about going from the penthouse to the outhouse. He was supposed to be playing for a national title. Now he'll be looking for a job to feed his family. Wow. What a disaster. Mike Ward must be devastated, too.

April 6

I have to admit, I'm having a ball. I've never enjoyed simply just coaching as much as I have this season. The kids are great. The team is coming together. We're developing a certain style—a semi-efficient offense and a devastating defense. All the boys are hustling, working hard, and playing team ball, like last year. We still have a ways to go, but I think we're a good edition. Our youngsters are growing up fast, our veterans are blending their talents, and the coaching situation is working out fine, better than I expected. Of course, we haven't had a crisis yet, as we surely will. Then, we'll see. I haven't given much thought to my future lately. I'm enjoying this year so much that I might want to come back as a consultant, if they want me. But they probably don't want me. Because if they wanted me, they already had me. Who is kidding whom?

April 11

We visit William Floyd in Mastic Beach on a warm Saturday morning. This is a South Shore blue-collar town, a total football-crazy town. They have great athletes and good lacrosse players every year, but not enough of them. The last time we saw the Colonials was our rain-soaked semi-final playoff win last year. Well, Andrew Miller is now a freshman at Johns Hopkins, so they presented a different challenge. We decided to cover their best attackman Justin Bunton with Westermann, our third defenseman. That freed up Kresse and DeVore to cheat the passing lanes and double on slides. My thought was if Westermann can contain the dodger, our beasts can roam free and plunder. And the strategy worked. Westermann played Bunton tough, blocking his every dodge, not throwing many checks but moving his feet, shutting him out, not even allowing an assist. Meanwhile Kresse and DeVore were all over the place, stealing forced passes, scooping dropped balls, DeVore picked up his second assist of the season. We were ahead 11-0 at the end of three quarters when we pulled our starters and coasted to a 12-3 victory.

Duggan saw limited duty on a sore ankle, but it didn't matter. Beltrani had a big game for us and our youngsters Pall, Molloy and Kunkel on attack played well enough—and gained valuable experience. Our senior middies Tsouris, Kelaher and Droesch get better each game, and they play so unselfishly. Junior Jono Feldman buried a high bounce-shot to register his first varsity goal. One bad note: Jason Smith (Ursinus), a junior middie with a good split-dodge, who has been coming into his own, got leveled by one of those football-players in a ground ball scrum and dislocated his collarbone. He will be out five weeks, minimum. After the game I went to see him in the hospital, to tell him how sorry I was, and how well he'd been playing. I wanted him to want to get back to us by the playoffs.

Driving home that night at dusk I figured out this was win four for the season, number 687 for the program. We have thirteen regular season games left and a probable playoff spot, which means we could make 700 if can duplicate or better last year's effort. We have a small margin of error.

Two losses, and we might still make it. More, though, this year has become about everybody who makes up Ward Melville lacrosse over the years, and what we have done together. I think of the great people who have worn the green-and-gold and I swell with pride. I've heard talk of a party to celebrate the success of the program if we make 700 wins. I think that sounds great and I let it be known I want it to be a family-style thing. Not some expensive thing at a catering hall.

We'll practice tomorrow afternoon, take Holy Thursday and Good Friday off. Get back to work on Saturday, then scout Chaminade at West Islip. Our league looks the way it usually does. West Islip, Northport and us seeded one, two, three—undefeated in the Division until we meet each other. We play a good Syosset team (6-0) on Monday afternoon and I always expect a tough game from a great Nassau Class A team.

Watching our guys at the college level, it's nice to see our 2005 boys doing so well. Ben-Eliyahu is having an amazing freshman year at Wesleyan. Giardinello starts at Suffolk CC and scored a pair of goals in their first-ever win over Nassau CC. Josh Blechman just won his first D-1 game between the pipes for VMI against Providence College. Nick Ward made the travel squad at Maryland. Brian Smith is a freshman middie at Lehigh. Will Konzcynin starts on defense as a sophomore at Stony Brook University for their up-and-coming head coach Lars Tiffany. Keegan Blaney and his brother Ryan play together at Marist. Mazzone, JP Mulhall and Ted Routi made the team at Siena College. Matt Rahner played club ball at University of Rhode Island and Jared Blechman played for the club team at the University of Michigan. Maurer took a redshirt year to heal his torn shoulder and will play next year at Towson. Alex Blechman also took a year off at Hobart to heal from a back injury. I have a lot of careers to follow, a lot of lives to care about.

We climbed to the twelfth spot in the national poll in Inside Lacrosse Magazine. I think we're better than that, and we'll get a chance to prove it.

April 15

Warm and sunny on income tax day. We practice for Syosset while West Islip beats Chaminade 10-6. All ten Lion goals came from their excellent attack of senior Kevin Federico (UNC), Justin Turri (Duke), a 6'3" junior, and another big junior 6'4" Brian Caufield (Albany), who scored also five goals against Chaminade. Meanwhile, in the 2006 Woodenstick Classic between Manhasset and Garden City, the oldest running high school rivalry in America, Doc Dougherty's Trojans stole another one, 15-14 in overtime.

Kaspar calls me at home and needles me, tells me his old Northport team is going to beat us bad on Wednesday because we don't have any offense. My gut is already in a knot because my gut suspects he might be right with Duggan still limping. But first things first. A very good Syosset team will be sky-high to whip us on Monday for regional pride alone, and we better go to Nassau County ready to brawl.

April 17

What a rotten day this was for us. Newsday ran a feature story about a winning high school baseball coach in Suffolk who was shoved aside when he retired from active teaching, so naturally they brought up my situation in the story, just when things have been going well. I'm pissed off about it, and I can tell Mike is pissed off the minute I see him get off the bus at Syosset. But there's nothing I can do about it and we have work to do and no time to quarrel. Syosset has a good team, but a team we should beat.

So, with the high school coaching world watching us because of the Newsday article, and our guys play like crap. Our captains are our worst offenders for boneheaded plays and a remarkable lack of focus. Young Rastivo does okay in the cage, but gives up a couple of softies. Our junior middies are clueless on defense, running around like puppies. DeVore has his only mediocre game as a high school player against Jeff Cohen, a junior attackman who will play at Harvard where his brothers starred. Westermann has to move out to long-stick middie to cover Matt Davie (UNC) because the juniors can't guard him. Tsouris and Droesch play well at d-middie, but we don't have many other bright spots. Everyone else is asleep for the noon start, or nervous and worried about themselves and their playing time. Our attack slips a lot. I mean they fall down and lose the ball behind their cage twenty times. I honestly thought they greased the grass at x, it was so JV-ugly, and still, somehow, with hustle and luck we're tied with a minute to go and possession of the ball. I suggested a time-out. Mike wanted to let it roll, to see how our boys handled it. I told him how they'd handle it. They're kids, playing an early season game. They'll blow it. And they did. We took a soft shot with 44 seconds left and hit the goalie on the strings of his stick, which turned into a fast break for them. DeVore got called for a hold near the sideline trying to contain the jailbreak. We started overtime man-down, and they had the ball. All-American attackman Chris Lubin isolated one of our short-stick middies behind the cage and blew past him for the game-winner. The Syosset kids ran onto their own field and whooped it up like they had won a state championship. That's what happens when you knock off the "most storied program" on Long Island. That's also what happens when we don't call time-out and set a strategy for emotional youngsters, each who thinks he's expected to be the hero. Well, sideline disagreements were bound to happen, and it could have gone the other way, too. I just hope we don't spread any more joy around this week. We go to Northport tomorrow, where the Island's best offensive unit goes to high school.

On the way home it dawned on me for the first time this season how much I missed being the only head coach, having my hands on the steering wheel. I also missed riding the team bus to the game and back to school and I vowed not to do that again. I have always coached on the bus. It's important that we ride as a team to the battle. All of us. That was my mistake. And I missed running the offense when things got bogged down. People think of me only as a defensive coach now, but for all those years Bill Martens was with us, I coached some pretty good attacks. And I really wanted to take that last time-out and call a set play. It's not like we've got Peyton Manning or Tom Brady running our offense. Anyway, I have some personnel changes in mind, but I think Mike does, too. I just hope they're the same ones.

Or I must learn to let go. And I don't want to let go.

April 18

We mix and match our offensive weapons, searching for a combo that works. Beltrani moves back to his natural position of right-handed attack and we shifted the sophomores down the depth-chart a bit until they have more maturity and seasoning. We also positioned Beltrani at X, where he says he is most comfortable, and we'll slide Duggan and Kunkel out to the wings, where they can rip away at the cage. Maybe that will work. But I'd rather switch Nagle, who never stops cutting, back to attack with Duggan and Kunkel. The other guys can play middie, or man-up. That's not my decision, but it's time for some of these guys to make themselves invaluable to us, or we'll keep losing close games. We owe it to everybody else that's been working so hard to win close games.

The high school threw a Spring Sports pep-rally and I think it helped us recover from our loss at Syosset. Morale seemed pretty good today among the boys at practice, although I still feel like an old sourpuss. I know, it is just one loss, a non-leaguer, means nothing, but it does. We are after perfection here.

April 19

Patriots' Day at Northport. At least that's what we're hoping. The Tigers are currently ranked sixth on Long Island and tenth in the country. They are also lopsided, not quite a mirror-image of our team. They are strong on offense, and shaky on defense. Newsday promoted the game with a preview suggesting it's the Empire kids from both teams against each other, but I know it will be more than that. The lifetime record stands at 40-3 in our favor but you can throw that out the window since 2001, when they won a state championship with Drew Thompson (UVA) and Kyle Dowd (Duke). They have a strong youth program, with superior coaching at the high school level from Bob Macaluso. I expect a hostile crowd on a hot, sunny afternoon. I expect media coverage, and I hope for a close game that we can steal at the end.

It is days like these—and great opponents like these—that make everything so exciting, so much fun. All year long I've talked barroom smack to my buddies Kaspar and Macaluso about us putting our fastest long-poles on Bartig and Chautin and Burr to stop them. I hope they have practiced for that configuration long and hard. Because that's exactly not what we're doing. On the bus ride to the game we decide to play them straight up. Am I crazy? I don't think so. We'll do it the same way it worked against William Floyd, even though Dowd is a bigger challenge for Westermann than Bunton. I've decided over the last few weeks that we don't have a one, a two, and a three defenseman. We have three number ones, and I can use them any way I want, mix and match them. Each has different strengths, but basically DeVore is a very strong, aggressive, slick takeaway artist, Kresse is a 230-lbs jackhammer who can run and hit, and Westermann is a lanky careful player who can run all day. He moves his feet and wears his opponents out.

Coach Macaluso watches us line up for the face-off and sees Westermann standing next to Craig Dowd and thinks I'm nuts. He immediately gives Dowd the green light, as if he didn't have it already. Dowd is a wide receiver/safety in football, a real gamer, and the younger brother of Duke star Kyle. All day long he isolates Westermann and takes it to him, from x, the corners, up top, time and time again, until late in the fourth quarter when both kids are clutching their shorts at time-outs. Our strategy is to fight that battle to a draw and let DeVore and Kresse overpower their two mere mortals. It wasn't fair, how well it worked. Tsouris and Droesch and

Kelaher accepted the challenge of guarding their good middies and did okay, good enough. Tsouris and Duggan scored a pair. JC Ward nailed a beauty waist-high for us, and all-purpose Nagle scored a big one to cinch the deal. We cut our turnovers in half, and held them scoreless for nearly twenty minutes in a brutal, hard-hitting second half. I mean, this was a brawl, bodies flying everywhere. Kelaher was laying down licks and grabbing ground balls. Just an awesome lacrosse game. Rastivo made some huge fourth quarter saves on Bartig, Burr and Dowd, who stole a clearing pass and attacked the cage one-on-none. Steve-o dropped to his knees to block a wicked sidearm shot down in the dirt from Burr with three minutes to go. Kunkel iced the game for us at 9-6 when he finished his hat trick in the fourth.

The Tigers walked off the field with a look of dismay on their faces, that we have done it to them again. Dowd got a pair of goals, one on a man-up play and one on a fast break, but he doesn't murder us in the six-on-six game like he has to everybody else the last few years. In spite of all the flashy resumes, Tsouris was the best midfielder out there. As I may have mentioned, Yale is getting one hell of a lacrosse player.

Ultimately, I think boys were ashamed of their loss to Syosset and responded with determination. Our offense did a decent job of controlling the ball and scoring. Our defense was aggressive and spirited against a star-studded line-up. A solid team effort, but still not enough to beat West Islip. If we don't get better on offense fast, the Lions are going to be tough to deal with. They are so fast and physical and smart. But first things first. We overlook nothing and take nothing for granted. West Babylon is next, on Friday night under the lights.

April 20

I wake up to see the first Newsday headline loving-up our goalie. Wanna bet he gets a few more on his way to All-American? A lot of our guys are bruised and limping today. I'm not surprised. Northport wanted to win badly and they played hard. Dowd threw big hits. Mike Mizvesky, too. Lynch. Burr. Bartig. Kelaher laid some wicked wallops on their middies and took a few in return, then went sliding through a pile on his knees to snatch an amazing ground-ball in the frantic fourth quarter. After watching the boys warm-up we decide to take it easy on them. We finalize Beltrani moving back to attack and shift the talented sophomore Pall to the third-line middies. Pall will have big days here at Melville, but Beltrani has earned his spot with hustle, a great change-of-direction, smart team play and selfless passing. Beltrani's got a couple more games at X against so-so opponents to get comfortable again before we need him to play great against West Islip and Yorktown. He's a quiet kid and he doesn't complain, even with all the position shifts, and learning new roles. Thank God he's so versatile. Like most of our boys, Alex is happy to contribute in whatever way we ask him to.

April 21

At Stony Brook University, we play the second game of a double-header. Our Patriot girls play first against undefeated East Islip. We have perhaps the best player in the US in her class here in Shaylyn Blaney. She is everything a great player should be and nothing they shouldn't be, just one of the best, hardest working kids you ever met.

In the national poll we are punished for our overtime loss to undefeated Syosset, and Northport is punished for losing to us. This looks like a year of balance, a group of teams bunched near the top. Massapequa. West Islip. Northport. Hicksville. Farmingdale. And us. It's a long season and it's not where you start, but where you finish. Tonight we play West Babylon. Next week, after the Commack road game, we play the #4 team in the country, our nemesis of the last four years, West Islip. Then we host the Yorktown Cornhuskers on Saturday. Our fate is in our own hands. We can earn back some of the respect we lost at Syosset or I can face a rotten final season here, a prospect too dismal to accept.

We get a nice night and a good crowd at LaValle after Shaylyn and the Patriot girls knock off undefeated East Islip. Once again, our defense is solid, not allowing a goal until a man-down situation late in the fourth quarter. And our offense is awful again, scoring only three goals in the first half and seven the entire game. We can't or won't shoot bounce-shots. Everything is fired sidearm and high. We can't hit the cage. We wind up and hit goalies in the belly. We stand around and watch each other lose the ball on dodges. We make a good defense look great. Mike Hoppey is really pissed at them tonight, and I don't blame him. He's got a rep as a great offensive coach and our guys are just killing him with bad play.

Saturday, April 22

We have a good practice inside the gym to warm up, and then go out in the rain for an intra-squad scrimmage. DeVore sits it out, resting a purple, swollen ankle. A couple of the younger guys sit out with nicks and bumps. That's okay. Rest is important, and they don't get enough of it in high school, not at the rate they are growing, and given the energy they expend.

In other action on Long Island Syosset goes to 9-0 and beats Massapequa 14-11, which makes our overtime loss to them hurt a little bit less. On a rainy night in Nassau poor Northport lost again, to Manhasset this time, 13-12, on a goal with two seconds left by Terence Molinari (Duke). What a rotten week for Macaluso and his Tigers. It'll be tough to pick them up on Monday after this, even though a non-league loss means nothing to their Class A Suffolk prospects. They better play Smithtown West tough on Tuesday night. If they lose that game, well, I'll be surprised if they do. I plan on being there to scout them both.

April 24

We give them a light workout again. Our defense knows its stuff by this time in a season and our offense is what it is. It's not a question of skills now but of confidence and chemistry. Lately I think practicing against our defense all the time has hurt their confidence as a unit more than toughened them to the task. They never get on a roll. They never get to let it rip. We end our workout early so our guys can walk over to the girl's field and root for Coach Erin Blaney and her kids against the fine Northport team led by Corrine Gandolfi and Megan Markowski. The Patriots lose to the Tigers 12-13 on a last second goal.

April 25

We get nice weather for our road trip to Commack, where our offense sputters again with lousy shooting for a quarter before Tsouris and Droesch dodge from the top and put a couple of standard-issue bounce-shots into the net. We lead 8-0 at the half and win 15-0. Senior Connor McCabe (Roger Williams) scores a goal. Junior Greg Brennan (Trinity) scores a goal. Pall and Timmy Golder (Scranton) as well. Our defense throws its first shutout since May 2004 against the Middle Country Mad Dogs. God, I love that mascot. Mad Dogs. Everybody plays against Commack. Tommy O'Connor has a strip and picks up a couple of ground balls. All three goalies record tough saves "Who bad?" someone yells as we turn into our high school driveway.

"We bad."

Back at Setauket, we quickly made our move from the high school locker room to LaValle Stadium to watch #2 Hofstra beat up on #19 Stony Brook 18-8. Former Patriots John Keysor, Ryan Kelaher, and Peter Kaspar play for John Danowski's Hofstra Pride. Will Konczynin starts on close defense for Lars Tiffany's Seawolves. Hofstra is loaded this year, a senior-laden team, with three Untersteins from Shoreham-Wading River to go with the Melville boys. The stadium is crowded with everybody from the local lacrosse scene, so it feels like old home week. People are buzzing about our Thursday game against West Islip. Do we have a chance to knock off # 4 in the country? I don't say anything, but I am considering some things our defense might surprise them with. Though I'll be surprised if our offense is up to the task. Maybe by late May—just not yet. I am a pessimist by nature and a worrier. I think most coaches are. Not that we tell our kids that.

April 26

The anticipation at our final practice before the West Islip match is delicious. I love big games and great opponents. I love it when a first-quarter balance settles in, and you know your boys are as good as theirs, that the game will go punch, counter-punch, punch. That it might come down to some coaching move, some last great notion or individual effort. We try not to kid ourselves in our game plan. We have flaws in our make-up, and we want them concealed and protected. We've got strengths and we want to leverage them. Smart, is what we need to be. Relentless. The way we played at Northport. The pasta party is at the Molloys' house tonight. I hope the boys eat well. I'll bet more than a few of them don't sleep so well. You think Christmas Eve is exciting to a six-year old? Not even close to this. Doesn't even register next to the tingling spines those starters will feel when the refs call them out to face the Lions. Give us a good start, I ask the Lord, if you've got time for lacrosse today, what with everything else that's wrong in the world. Don't make us play those bastards from a hole.

April 27

Newsday gives the West Islip game another big promotion, the same old same old, DeVore and Kresse against the Evil Empire. The reporter actually calls them the Dynamic "D-uo." And they are, no kidding. But defense is a team game, so it's a good thing Colin Field, Tsouris, Droesch, Westermann and Rastivo don't mind being left out, or at least they don't complain. Especially since Tsouris might be the best defensive middie we've ever had play at Melville and every college coach in the country is following Rastivo's rapid development. I've been in hundreds of these big games and each one is special. The adrenaline pump is cranking, and I don't know what to do with myself until game time. Then I'll know. Until then I'll read the paper. I'll watch CNN and MSNBC and Fox. I'll workout. Eat. Pace the floor. We can beat these guys, if we play our best. And if we can beat these guys, we'll have something to build on this year. Half the job is convincing your own team that they're the best sons of bitches that ever walked out onto that field in green-and-gold.

So what do we do? We go out and score but one lousy goal in a sloppy first half, and give up four bad ones. Our young middies don't even attempt to cover their men and we pay, repeatedly. Didn't matter that Westermann shut out Federico, the all-time point-scorer in West Islip history, that Kresse hammered his kid, and also had a huge assist to spark a minor comeback, that DeVore shut out Justin Turri (Duke). The Lions have the ball almost the whole damn game, and we don't crack. And still we lose. West Islip scored only two second-half goals and we lost! Our offense turned the ball over ten times before they even got a shot on the cage. Christian Scuderi (NYIT), Anthony Florido, Derek Speziale (Albany) and Ryan Flanagan (UNC) swallowed them alive. It was hard to watch. We ended the game with possession of the ball for the last fifty seconds and didn't get a shot off. Not one measly dribbler. How does that happen? I can't remember when I've been madder, but I don't say a word. My sphere of influence is limited and I'm choking.

Mike Hoppey has incredible patience with some of the kids we have running around out there not playing defense on their men. I think it's time to shrink our line-up and send people to the bench. They will play next year, or the year after, when they're stronger, faster, with better skills and sense of the game. They've seen what it's like up here and they've seen what they need to do to improve. Great. Mission accomplished. No more on-the-job training. We need to season a squad for the playoff run. There's a huge opportunity here.

I talked to West Islip head coach Scotty Craig before the game and we both agreed that the winner of Suffolk County had a good chance to win it all in New York State. West Genny has been in several close games in its section, and might be slightly down for a change. Massapequa has flaws, but not many. Syosset we already know, and we think we can beat them in a rematch. Maybe John-Jay in Section I is in a good position to win it, or if a young Yorktown grows up in a hurry. We'll see. I still like the Suffolk Champ to go all the way.

Leaving the parking lot after the game I'm beginning to feel like I won't be here next year, and it's going to be different but okay. I find I don't have the same feel for this younger class that I do for my seniors—and the fault belongs to me. I think once I knew the team wasn't all mine anymore, I began to mentally detach, to use the back door to come and go. What's that expression? Nobody washes a rented car? It's an awful feeling.

April 28

Northport beat Smithtown West 9-7 in a night game at West, but the Tigers lost their star middie Max Bartig with a badly pulled hamstring. He lay at midfield and groaned in frustration, indicating he'll be out for a while. In the stands we learned that West Genny lost in triple-overtime. Scotty Craig must be feeling really good about his chances tonight. The Droesch/Redko pasta party was tonight out on Strong's Neck, and they invited me to come, which was nice. I have never attended a pasta party, and I thought about going, but I had dinner plans with Lucretia. When I put it that way, the guys understand. They like that I'm not alone every night out east.

We get no punishment in the national poll for dropping a one-goal game to the #3 team in the country. Of course, now we have to run the table to get to 700 wins. We have to win the rest of the regular season games and two additional playoff games. Otherwise, we'll fall one win short at 699. What does that mean in the long run? I don't know. Is it just a number? I haven't faced it.

April 29

Yorktown at Ward Melville lacrosse means a boy-girl doubleheader on a sunny spring day. If there's a Heaven, it's got great lacrosse rivalries like this one. After the games, everybody will sit down together and eat in the cafeteria, referees and parents, too. Future college teammates will connect. Faces go with names. We have an advantage in the series record, but the games are usually hard-fought and close in score. They have three All-American candidates on their roster, Tommy Interlicchio (Hofstra) on the midfield, Kyle Vercruysse (Siena) on defense, and Jake DeLillo (NYIT) at attack, but I think our guys can handle them. I hope we can generate some offense, or at least not embarrass ourselves in front of the Section I folks. Hell, I grew up in Section I.

I'm pleasantly surprised as we cruise to a 13-4 win and get just about everybody into the game. We jumped up 8-1 at the half, and pulled the starters with a 12-2 lead in the third period. Kelaher scored three goals and three assists from his new position at attack. Duggan and Kunkel each got two goals. Junior middie Jeff Routi earned some playing time this week and made it pay with a goal and some open-field hits. He'll see more action this week, looking to replace some of Kelaher's toughness between the lines. My senior defensemen did their usual work and allowed nothing. Nada. Hardly let them get a shot off. They are uncanny, maybe the best group we've ever had play together here. Certainly they are the best ball-handlers, as a unit, ever. (And we've had many great defenders, including but not limited to: Bob Rotanz (Roanoke) and Tom Rotanz, Kevin O' Shea, Jon Fox (UNC), Chris Walker (UNC), Joe Junior, Harold Drumm (UMass), Matt Grosso (Brown), Chris Passavia (Maryland), Ryan Kelaher (Hofstra), Andrew Maurer (NYIT.)

After the lunch—served by our parents—in our cafeteria, Mike Hoppey gave a sportsmanlike speech to send the Huskers on their way. It's been a great rivalry and I hope it continues after I'm gone. Many of our alumni attend the game and the lunch, and what fun it is to watch '97 State Champs Anthony Pisciotto (Salisbury), Mike Monfett (Brown) and Rich Kunkel (UMass) assure our present-day defenders that they could have indeed, before they grew bellies, tool them, school them and toast them bad. DeVore, Kresse and Westermann look at those pot-bellies and receding hairlines and think the boasting is ludicrous, even though they look up to these guys. Me, I don't know who'd win that battle. It might depend on which side I coached—just kidding.

The boys get a day off tomorrow and they need it. I see limping again after lunch, boys moving very slowly to leave. Meanwhile West Islip whips Section I Mahopac 11-5, and Kevin Federico scores six goals to get himself re-started. Our potential downstate adversary, if we get that far, John Jay—Cross River, beats Garden City 15-11. They have already beat Yorktown 11-7 in their annual slugfest. So I'm guessing they are pretty good.

The news about me coaching in the Under Armour game comes out, and of course I'm pleased by this honor. It means a lot to me that people all over the country know and respect what we have accomplished here.

May 1

On Guam, we come out flat against a tough East Islip team. We've got college coaches in the stands and we can't get our seniors off the field to showcase the younger guys. I see the junior parents squirming, watching their dreams for their sons tick away. Recruiting happens so early now, especially for the top teams with only 12.3 scholarships spread out over four years. Brown's Jon Thompson is at the game with a clipboard to watch Westermann (their freshman next year) and our sophomores and juniors with good grades. He only gets a good look at Rastivo, Kunkel and Field because we struggle on offense again. But I already know that Brown would like to land Rastivo. It's the other guys that don't get a look.

This is a frantic time of year in recruiting. Parents beg me to talk to the Princeton guy, the Hopkins guy, the Duke guy or the Georgetown guy. But the best D-1 programs aren't there to pluck our tenth player or even our fifth player. They want the best guy available (with good grades), the guy the rest of our league has to worry about. They want our standouts. But some school wants almost everybody. To make our team makes you attractive. The top college coaches scout our league and I've come to admire quite a few of them. Besides former Ward Melville players who are now head coaches in the college ranks (Jim Nagle at Colgate and Chris Wakely at Lehigh), I'm very fond of Bill Tierney at Princeton. Bill's a salty old Cortland guy like me, and has turned a so-so Tiger lacrosse program into a great national power. He can get a little excited on the sideline, but, hey, so can I. We care. So sue us. His players and their parents think the world of him and he knows how to win.

I love Dom Starsia, now at the University of Virginia after a decade at Brown. Mike Pressler is a hell of a coach and good man, and I'm rooting for him to bounce back. Seth Tierney (Hofstra head coach) is going to be terrific. Seth played for Jimmy Kaspar at McArthur High School, and is Bill's nephew. He was a great offensive assistant at Johns Hopkins before replacing John Danowski, another Long Island guy. Tom Leanos at Drew University, where at least one Ward Melville boy has been on the roster most of the last twenty-five years. And I love Siena's Brian Brecht (Sachem) who is a first class recruiter and tactician. I expect a lot out of him in the future. Fred Acee at Air Force. The list goes on.

Anyway, thank God Colin Field and Kresse scored goals with their long-poles to make it 9-3 or it would have been even worse. We gave up two of their three goals on man-down plays, but still . . . I see us as a team adrift, going nowhere, tinkering with the line-up at the halfway mark. Routi, who looked so good and tough against Yorktown, had a bad day on the defense end and was returned to the sideline. JC Ward, who saw his minutes limited against Yorktown, played better defense against East Islip, so he stayed in the game. We need his stick skills and physical talent. He's a good two-way football player who likes to mix it up. Next year he'll be huge for this team, a leader or captain. Some of the other juniors are absolutely clueless, and I'm almost glad I won't have to coach them. I've climbed the learning curve with so many classes. Some have been better than others. So many blend together in my mind.

After the game one junior's visibly upset father asked Mike Hoppey why his son wasn't playing, and Mike pulled him aside to explain. It made me recall all the times parents have come to the high school principal or gone to the school board meeting to publicly question my judgment. Lawyers, doctors, plumbers, pilots—you name it. All of them are lacrosse experts. I usually ask them how long they've been coaching lacrosse and at what level. I tell them I would never have the nerve to go to their place of business and tell them how to do their jobs. Some understand, and apologize. Some never do. Mike is pretty upfront with this particular disappointed dad. I hear him say the kid will play when he decides to stop turning the ball over, plays some defense and has some clue as to what's going on around him on the field. The dad slinks away, chastened. He loves his kid, and thinks he's a great player, but it takes a lot to get on the field for us and stay there. You have to contribute, make plays, help us win, not just survive unharmed or unnoticed.

Meanwhile, in other news, Sachem East upsets an excellent Smithtown West team 8-5. Looks like coach Rick Mercurio has got his team playing well at the right time.

May 3

We go to Lindenhurst on the South Shore on a miserable rainy night to play on their new Field Turf. DeVore sits out with a pulled hammy and sophomore Matt Spagnoli (Bucknell) starts in his place. Matzelle (CW Post) starts in goal to give Rastivo a break, and Jon plays well, as I knew he would. He could start almost anywhere in our league, and he's a great kid, who handled the arrival and anointing of Rastivo with courage and grace, always put the team first. I wish everybody on this team was as willing to sacrifice for others as Jon. I wish Jon played another position because I'd love his attitude and toughness on the field for us.

We win 18-3 as our offense finally explodes. Brian Brecht, the Siena coach, was there to watch his recruits Duggan and Timmy Rau, a nifty attackman from Lindy. Kunkel scores six goals and Duggan plays well and scores twice. But Westermann and Kresse hang a smothering o-o on Rau. To be fair, Rau doesn't have much to work with, and no one to set him up. I suspect Brecht appreciates that.

Even though it's a miserable night in the bleachers, West Islip head coach Scott Craig is in the stands, making notes on his clipboard. His team hammered Connetquot 20-4 earlier in the day, but the big man is on a mission. He is watching us, stalking us. He knows that on any given day we can beat them and ruin everything.

May 4

We elevate sophomore Josh La Mantia into our midfield rotation of six. He's very fast and plays real hard and the junior boys ahead of him have failed to secure the position. That's how it goes here. Everyday is a tryout day with so many good players waiting for a chance. Mike Hoppey has played a lot of underclassmen this year, more than I would have. I don't see all-out effort from a lot of them, and I get a sense of entitlement from some I don't think they've earned. All this on-the-job training we've allowed could hold Mike in good stead next year, as he'll have some experienced players coming back. It gives me more gray hair.

May 5

I hate the waiting for night games, but I love the adrenaline pump. We have a girls' game ahead of ours, a parent's tailgate in the parking lot, and a rowdy crowd of students on hand. I hear via the grapevine that West Islip is ahead of Northport at the half 5-2 and that Higbie Lane outside West Islip High School is packed with cars. That's about what I expected on a warm Friday night in May. West Islip eventually wins it 13-6. The big man is on a mission.

DeVore suits up to see if his sore hamstrings will allow him to hang with the Smithtown West creaseman Jaime Rogers. Jake and Matt will handle their speedy feeders and dodgers, Scott Perri (Drexel) and Rob Pannell (Cornell), two first-class juniors. The have middies Brad Burton and Brian

Smalley (Loyola) and Tom Walsh (Ursinus), lots of weapons. And a good defense. So I'm nervous. These Smithtown West offensive guys are sneaky good. I need another "A" game from my defensive troops. And some Patriot offense at the other end would be nice.

What we got was the worst display of offensive lacrosse I've ever seen on that field. Turnover after turnover. We can't dodge. Can't catch. Can't pick up a ground ball. Kunkel gets three goals but everyone else disappears with the game on the line. Smithtown's defense is good, but not this freaking good. And Smithtown's attack is relentless, running, cutting, forcing tension on every possession. Something's got to give, you can see it coming. We stumble into overtime tied at four. Westermann slides to an open middie and gets a thirty-second push call from Kenny Rizzo, one of the great referees. Westermann goes to the penalty box and never gets on the field again, because only a short stick can return when his time is served, as we already have four poles on the field. With less than two minutes left, Pannell dodges down the left slot and buries a rocket low in the far corner. Steve-o never had a chance. Game over. Our crowd sits there dead, embarrassed for us.

It's hard to know what to say. Home field for the playoffs, a good chance at 700 wins is now an outside chance, momentum heading into the playoffs—all squandered at home. I've never seen us play so crappy on offense—we look like beginners. We throw flat-footed, casual passes. Also, I think Smithtown West wanted that game more than we did. So I am frustrated beyond words. Our defense needs to be perfect in close games if we hope to win. Our offense affords us such a small margin of error.

Look, I believe we are one of the better teams in our division. But this is a critical part of the season. We desperately need to get better, fast. But the schedule is set up in our favor, giving us an opportunity to go into the playoffs off four straight wins. It falls on us as coaches to get these guys to step up when it counts. What we can do to save this season? Win the county. With what? I don't know.

Some guys never understand that their early shot-on-goal may be the most important play of the game. Their bad passes count, add up. The blown clear. The soft ride. They cost us. We don't know what's going to happen next. No one does. After a bad play, we can say to each other, "No problem. We'll get it back," but maybe we won't. Maybe we've blown it. Seasons are like that, too, wrecked before you know it. I'm not sure this team has the discipline and urgency to go all the way. Maybe we don't think we can do it. I always tried to set up a certain state of mind, even against lesser opponents. We want to be consistent and professional, business-like winners. When we arrive at an away game we form two straight lines and march from the bus to the field in serious silence. I have always told the boys, if the home team stops their warm up and watches us enter the field, we've got them intimidated. And I'm usually right.

I will say this in the team's defense: There is tremendous pressure on our kids to win every game, to uphold the Patriot reputation. And a lot of our fans don't give our opposition any credit. If we lose, it's always: What's wrong with Ward Melville? But other Long Island programs have good players and work hard, too. This Smithtown West team is an excellent lacrosse team, full of Division I talent. Next year they might win it all. Kevin Huff had a lot to do with building this West team before moving to East to start up a new, and already successful, program without any seniors. He's such a good coach, he made the playoffs with that young group, too. A star middie at Hofstra in his playing days, he is just the most respectful, polite, hardworking guy, even after he's beaten us.

Speaking of talented opposition—West Islip is loaded with players going to North Carolina, Duke, Albany, Towson, Robert Morris and NYIT. This year they might win the county for the third year in a row. Bob Macaluso's Northport team has those Under Armour All-Americans and a solid supporting cast—and he added an All-County goalie Scott Dale to his line-up. So it's not chopped liver we're playing here. Many Long Island high schools have admirable lacrosse traditions. Ours has just been a little bit better.

Mike Hoppey gave our guys the weekend off after the game. I would have brought them back to school at dawn to run for hours, but then I'm a miserable bastard. No wonder they showed me the door. Good God, I'm mad. Nobody should ever want to win more than we do, especially at home. We've allowed 3.7 goals a game this season and are on the ropes. We are three goals away from an undefeated season, and reeling.

May 7

It is a beautiful day and I wish we were practicing. Massapequa beat Niskayuna easily yesterday, again pointing to Long Island's relative strength this year—if we could only be a player in the dance. Overnight internet griping about our loss to Smithtown West lays the blame for the lousy offense on Coach Hoppey, but that's counter-productive. We are not out of this race, not by any stretch. Patriot teams come back when we're behind. We get up when we get knocked down. Not all of those 690-some wins were cakewalks. Some of them were gut-wrenching, last-second surprises, even to me, though I tried to never let that show. I know my defense won't need help to get themselves up. I sense no let-up in their desire to dominate, so I trust they will keep us in every game. But I worry the offense has lost their confidence. And I worry the two ends of the field will bitch at each other. I worry that players might turn selfish if our team goals are lost. I worry all the time.

May 8

I say we need to start over. Or start thinking like it's the playoffs already, our backs against the wall, one loss and we're done. We need to play with urgency. One loss and high school lacrosse is over, boys. Kaput. For you and for me. Nothing but a fond memory. You'll be college freshmen on teams that don't know you or need you or trust you. Ponder that. At practice I tell the defense from now on they have to limit the opposition to two goals per game, and they don't get that I'm kidding. They nod earnestly and promise me, you got it, coach. We need DeVore's legs to really heal if we're going to hold anybody to two goals a game. And it wouldn't hurt to get Jason Smith back healthy. He was playing well when he went down against Floyd. Like Tsouris and Droesch, Jason can get himself his own shot.

On the internet, which is a relatively new phenomenon for old coaches like me, all the petty agendas are in play. Parents are angling for playing time for their boys, usually with digs against unproductive starters. There is an attempt to divide the coaches into my fans against Mike's fans. This stuff all used to be done in the barbershops and hardware stores on 25A, on the driving range at St. George's Golf Club, or over the bar at Mario's or the Checkmate. Nowadays opinionated Patriot fans flow to the Newsday and LaxPower chat-rooms and sound off anonymously as if they are experts. More than ever I am constantly reminded: Because we are a high visibility program, when we lose, people want to know why. And not everyone wishes us well.

May 9

At Connetquot we face a Thunderbird team that has struggled this year after graduating a good class in 2005. Their best big middie, Mark Leggerio, is a rugged football player headed to Lafayette—but to play football. He scored six goals against Sachem East last week, so we know we have to guard him. And we do, first with Tsouris, then Field, then Westermann. Leggerio gets tired and gets nothing. It's a 17 to 1 win for us as the Ward Melville offense arrives a game late.

Today the boys were moving without the ball and passing unselfishly. LaMantia made the sweetest pass of the day, a feed across the crease when everyone thought sure he would shoot. We need more of that. LaMantia also scored a goal, as he earns more playing time with his speed and attitude. Kelaher was shooting through screens from everywhere and couldn't miss. In fact, Kelaher personally chased their starting goalie with ninety-mile-per-hour rockets. DeVore sat out again, frustrated, with two sore hammies. Meanwhile Kresse was a stripping machine and Westermann and Field led the team in groundballs. Everybody on both ends got playing time. Kunkel scored five goals, and Duggan four. Brennan added a pair. JC Ward and McCabe scored again. I had told the defense they could only give up two goals a game, and they only allowed one, a funky bounce-shot Rastivo overran. Anyway, I think we got some of the bad taste out of our mouths from the Smithtown West game. We travel to Sachem North on Thursday, the other half of what was once our greatest rivalry.

May 11

We jump ahead 10-1 at the half at Sachem North, and coast to an easy 15-1 victory on Fred Fusaro Field. DeVore sits out again and everybody else plays, but again our offense is bad early, with dropped passes, stolen passes, pipes hit, you name it. The fifteen goals would have been thirty if we could finish a fast break. Kunkel gets five more, and is on a serious scoring binge, one of the best shooters in the county. Tsouris gets himself a pair. Greg Sefarian, wearing a big knee-brace, wins some face-offs for us and scores a nice goal. We now own win # 695, which means we need take the next two regular season games and three playoff games—which means we have to win the county championship game. Not just appear in it and lose.

Meanwhile, West Islip clobbers Sachem East 15-0. The Lions are now ranked #3 in the country by the LaxPower Poll and Inside Lacrosse Magazine. We're slotted at #70. So there's room to move up.

May 12

It was pouring rain outside today, so we worked in the gym. We ran sprints, a lot of them, did a little stick-work. The boys are feeling better about themselves after a couple of easy wins, but nobody is swaggering, everybody still chastened by the Smithtown West defeat. We hand out the schedule for Senior Day on Monday. The parents of our seniors will join their sons on the field before the game as we thank them for their contributions and announce the colleges they will play for next spring. I am happy and proud and sad all at once. Win, lose, or draw, from here on out, whether we make it to 700 or more or fall short, this dogged group has become in my mind representative of all the other Patriots teams. They have earned that much with their very hard work. Great players, great students, great friends to each other. Anything is possible.

May 13

We schedule a 10 AM practice to keep the boys away from the temptation of Three Village beer blasts. We run them hard, then send them home to rest. That evening Manhasset knocks off John Jay—Cross River in overtime 13-12. Only West Islip remains undefeated at the top of New York State. And they only beat us by a goal. We have such possibilities, if we can only get a little better.

May 15

Rain poured down on the scheduled Senior Day, so we moved the game to tomorrow afternoon. Then the sun came out, so we practiced outside and worked up a good sweat. Inside Lacrosse magazine threw Ward Melville and West Genny out of the national Top 25 at the same time for the first time since I can remember. Boys' Latin retained the top spot. They were followed by Georgetown Prep, West Islip and Huntington. Three one-goal losses and we're suddenly stumblebums. I look at that Top 25 list and I know there are teams we could beat. No matter. West Islip is still sitting top five. And I know we can beat them.

May 16

We should have played Middle Country yesterday. The sun came out and the field dried up . . . reminds me of the unnecessary rainout last year of the county finals—how ready we were to play. I recall the bus accident on the way back to Melville. Everyone tense, snapping at each other. The bitter 6-3 loss two days later still stings. Today it is pouring again, the field a sea of mud. So we cancel again. Then it is sunny again.

There are always bumps and bruises, even during the undefeated years. We rely on our mental toughness, how we react and endure, how we stick together through everything. We will now play at Sachem East on Thursday and close out our regular season Friday against Middle Country. Then we'll get really busy, working harder than ever at practice, at least that's what I've always liked about playoff time. First-year varsity players are shocked at the increase in intensity, the scouting and planning. They get sore again, after thinking they were in tip-top shape.

If we're going to make anything special of our joint farewell to Ward Melville, we need to do it in the playoffs. The regular season has been a disappointment to everyone. When I looked at our line-up in the preseason, I thought we'd be better. Maybe people now understand how good Giardinello was at beating defensemen one-on-one, how important Ben-Eliyahu's toughness and hands were to last year's team. What Maurer meant to our team attitude, also the outside shooting of Nick Ward and Alex Blechman. We never replaced those things and we missed them.

May 17

We practice for my last visit to Sachem East, or any Sachem for that matter. This has been such a great rivalry over the years. One-goal games, double-overtimes, huge comebacks, wild crowds, with a dash of class warfare. Our supposedly "pampered rich kids" against their supposedly "tough blue-collar" kids. At least that's how they saw it. The game will be filmed and televised next week. I hope that doesn't throw the boys. They have some good players, as always, but nobody this year like Pat Perritt, now a freshman at Syracuse. We should win this game comfortably. Famous last words, I know. I hear the boys have their pasta party down on the beach in Stony Brook this evening. Ah, the Three Villages. Great place to raise a kid.

May 18

A sunny morning dawns on Long Island and the playing fields are drying out. Sachem East is ready for us. But we are not ready for them. They score a bad-bounce goal to get started, and we break for the half down 3-2. And we have stunk up the joint again on offense. Again! Soft, dumb lazy. What is it when we come to play here? I can't watch it anymore.

So at halftime I snapped. I mean, I ripped our kids like they haven't been ripped in a year. I cursed them, questioned their manhood, their talent, heart and brains, their choices for college. I told them they were an embarrassment to every team that ever wore the green-and-gold. They dropped their heads and stared at the grass, some of them mumbling curses at themselves and at me. I know I've mellowed over the years, but there still has to be some penalty for bad play, taking shots into the goalie's stick that wind up fast breaks headed the other direction. A coach can be too understanding, too easy going. We can play harder and smarter. I know we can.

The boys got spitting mad at me, and stormed out on the field, pissed. They served up an angry 9-1 second half on a startled Sachem East squad, and I decided I or someone else needed to go berserk a little more often. After the 11-4 win, Kresse told me he loved it when I yelled at people, even if it was at him. "We miss that fear factor this year," he said. "No one is afraid."

May 19

The parents aren't always complaining.

> Dear coach,
>   It's Senior Day and I just wanted to say having my son play for you was everything we hoped for. Of all the people he's met at Ward Melville, you have had by far the most positive influence. He was saying he'd like to play two more years before going to college. I asked if he really wanted to play on next year's team. His friends will be gone. You will be gone. It won't be the same. I told him he had played for the country's best lacrosse coach and he had much to be proud of. Time to move on.
>
>   Sincerely,

It's raining again. Middle Country has their Junior Prom tonight, so we're an early start at 3:30. We decide to do the Senior Day ceremony at halftime. Then the playoff committee can get about their seedings, and we can focus in on the job at hand. I like the way we played in the second-half against Sachem East. I like the way they responded to the whip. Other players besides Kresse told me later, thank God you finally yelled. They thought something was wrong with me or they were losing their minds, I'd been so quiet and nice this year. I guess I really am feeling sad and emotional as the season nears completion. So many milestones have come and gone, and so few remain. Last Senior Day, last home game, last playoff run. There have been moments of great frustration serving as a co-coach, especially when decisions were made with which I did not agree. But still I'm glad I did it. Our personalities and coaching styles are so different. Mike is laissez-faire, where I'm a control-freak. I think if you screw up you should sit a while and stew, learn the lesson. Mike thinks you get a second chance, a third chance, more encouragement. Both styles can work, just maybe not side-by-side. Still, I'm glad I came back, and I will walk away with my head held high. I know I can still coach and still get the best from kids. These seven student-athletes that make up my defense this year are my real legacy. I'll match them with anyone's.

After two previous rainouts, Middle Country made the short trip up Nicolls Road.

Mike Hoppey and Will Gray joined me on the field as I, along with seventeen seniors, "graduated" from Ward Melville. I kept my face blank, I hope. This is no time for me to feel sorry or draw attention to myself. I want to finish strong.

Middle Country (5-7) is in the middle of Division I, on the bubble for the playoffs. They beat Brentwood 18-7 on Wednesday, sparked by a four-goal performance by senior Ryan Fitzgerald. They need to upset us to earn a playoff berth or their season is over. After seven tense scoreless minutes Kelaher ripped top shelf through a screen to put us on the board. Droesch fed Kunkel for a nifty behind-the-back shot to make it 2-0. Middle Country's Tyler Hope dodged from the wing and scored in the top right corner to make it 2-1. But Kunkel scored again almost immediately, unassisted. Beltrani made it 4-1. Greg Sefarian won the ensuing face-off, which set up another goal by Kelaher just as the thunder rumbled in and the game was suspended. This is surreal, the game that will not end, and strangely I don't mind.

I could stand on this field and do this forever.

May 20

The teams returned to Ward Melville on Saturday morning to complete the contest. We hugged the senior boys and gave the dads their Patriot hats and their moms their flowers before we got started again, just in case anything else happened and we had to run for the building. Middle Country got off to the faster start as Vinny Sandtorv dodged from the midfield and scored unassisted to make it 5-2. Todd Dermody made several saves for them to close out the first-half.

Kelaher got fully warmed up in the second half, adding two more assists and a goal to pad our lead. Duggan finished an assist from Droesch. Kunkel found the net again and JC Ward added the final Melville tally. The final of 11-4 put us into the playoffs with a first-round bye.

After the game we talked to the team. The previous evening the Suffolk Lacrosse Coach's handed out the post-season awards and seeded the County tournament. The coaches made Kresse an All-American and DeVore an Honorable Mention All-American, which will shock a few people. Both are great players and both had great seasons, but Sam missed games with injury and it cost him. Westermann earned All-Division and All-County honors, as did Tsouris—who was probably our best all-around player this year. Kelaher and Duggan were All-County. Tsouris and Westermann were nominated for Academic All-Americans, as their weighted grade-point averages are an identical 4.9555s. Kunkel made All-Division, which had to be a disappointment, considering he led the team in scoring. Rastivo was Suffolk County Class A Rookie of the Year. About an average year for Ward Melville, which isn't bad. God knows. I'm not complaining.

2006 Playoffs

May 22

A nice day out, with a peppy intra-squad scrimmage. We give the starting defense the third midfield and third attack and the split squad plays a practice game. The first D-guys win it in overtime. Then our All-Everythings have to jump in their cars and race to Hauppauge High to have their mug shots taken with Suffolk's other stars. This is a great time of year, filled with recognition of past accomplishments and the anticipation and tension of big games to come. We've got a first-round bye, then play the winner of the East Islip/Lindenhurst game on Thursday at home. I expect it will be East Islip. They have more weapons.

My pal Jimmy's Kaspar's Long Beach Marines go down swinging in the Nassau A playoffs after a truly great year for a bunch of kids nobody knew about. If that was not a Coach of the Year performance by Jimmy, I don't know what is.

May 25

We won our regular season meeting 9-3, but today the Redmen changed offensive strategy and were tough on defense for a solid first half. Thank God Nick Tsouris won the opening face-off for us and raced downfield to score in only twelve seconds. Tsouris won the next face-off and Kelaher set up Kunkel for a quick-stick. After another Tsouris win, Ward poured a laser past the goalie's leg to give us a quick 3-0 lead.

Early in the second quarter Kresse led a clear that ended with Kelaher feeding Duggan to give us a four-goal margin. East Islip didn't fold. They responded with a pair of goals off unsettled situations and were happy to break for at the half down 4-2. I didn't feel comfortable letting them hang around, and I told the boys so.

Early in the third East Islip's All-County attackman Brett Djaha scored on a cut through the crease and our four-goal lead dwindled to one. Tsouris responded with an unassisted goal to make it 5-3. Nagle plucked a rebound out of the air and buried an insurance goal to stretch the lead to three. Tsouris scored again, unassisted, then Beltrani dunked a rebound. Kunkel stole a clearing pass and scored and the Redmen were broken, with the final score 10-3. But it was closer than it looked. They couldn't dodge our poles so they inverted their offense and took our short-stick middies behind the cage. Tsouris, Droesch, Ward and LaMantia all did a great job playing man-to-man defense back there. Still, it was close for a while. Our depth and conditioning wore them down, as it should have. Now we re-visit second-seeded Northport on Tuesday at 4PM. Their great offense against our great defense, one more time.

I heard a funny story this afternoon: Big Russ Rastivo pulled up outside the gym to pick up Steve-o after the game. Some of our senior starters were hanging on the sidewalk, expecting to be congratulated for beating East Islip. Russ saw them grinning and rolled down his window. "Hey, fellas," he said. "Take that clown act to Northport next Tuesday and we can put away the gear for the year."

Russ told me their jaws dropped. Steve-o hung his head in shame. Me, I threw back my head and cackled. I would have loved to see their faces. Poor babies win a playoff game and the parents crap all over them. What a town.

Big Russ is right. We play like clowns at Northport on Tuesday and they will kick our butts out of this tournament. Three Northport players (Craig Dowd, Max Bartig and Max Chautin) have been selected to participate in the Under Armour All-America game. Sam DeVore and I will represent Ward Melville at Towson University on June 18th.

May 26

No school today, to make up for the lack of snow-days this winter. Lack of snow days? They're kidding, right? It was always snowing this winter, it seemed. We practice at 10AM to get them up and out of bed early. We need more work on our offense. How can we still need so much work this late? I want these playoffs to go on forever, because when they're over, I know I'm done here.

May 27

I sense our guys are physically tired. Westermann and Field limp like old men. DeVore kept himself out of practice with both hammies flaming. Kresse has a big fat purple ankle. Rastivo is always ready to work, and I am more impressed than ever with him as the season progresses. Not just the great saves, or outlet passes, or his sense of calm out there when things get hairy. He's already a man in a skinny sophomore body. Our seniors love him, look out for him, and have promised Big Russ they won't let him get "lit up." So far they have kept their word. He sees about nine shots a game and averages six saves.

We give the guys tomorrow off and tell them to rest, and I mean rest. Feet up, do nothing. Eat well and sleep. I want them strong on Tuesday—quick on their feet, quick as they have ever been in their lives.

For lacrosse fans this is the best weekend of the year. The NCAA Final Four is going on. The Long Island high school tournaments have reached the serious stage. You don't want to be done playing when this weekend rolls around. You want to feel a part of it, like you're just beginning your season. We still have two Ward Melville boys alive in the Final Four in Philly. Nick Ward at Maryland and Tommy Theodorakis at Syracuse. And by the afternoon we have none. UMass will play Virginia on Monday. Drew Thompson plays for Virginia. He captained Northport's state championship team in 2001. We play at dangerous Northport again on Tuesday. Lose and it's over. Thirty-eight years at an end. Spring is in the air, I notice.

May 28

I pray for one more victory over Macaluso. I need it this year, more than he does. Of course I usually think like that. At the strangest times this season I have found myself emotional about other things, things that end: like soldiers and summers and friendships. I would have done this for free, if anyone had asked, until I couldn't walk out to Guam anymore. I have been a proud father, husband and teacher, but this place and this game have defined me to the outside world.

May 29

On Memorial Day I pray for lost soldiers and I pray for peace. We practice at 10AM again, and I pray this is not my last morning on this field. The NCAA Championship game is on ESPN at 1PM. Over 40,000 turned out on Saturday in Philadelphia for the semifinals. Our little game has grown in the last forty years . . . since we played with wooden sticks. It is stronger and more vibrant than at any time I can remember. I wish I felt as young and strong and vibrant. My way of dealing with my feelings of loss as the end of the season draws close is to pull even closer with my guys on defense. I'm so proud of how hard they have played for me these last two years. They are closing in on the lowest goals-allowed-average on Long Island for a second straight year.

May 30

Hot, sunny, the afternoon going to be muggy. We told the boys to start drinking water last night and all day and we need to re-hydrate on the thirty-minute bus ride to Northport, even if everyone has to run into the school and pee the minute we get there. Our bench strength won't matter much today, because we won't use them unless we have to. This is to stay alive, and we can't afford rookie mistakes. We need to keep our main horses watered.

The stands will be full of college coaches, guys on their way home from the NCAA Finals in Philly. It's too bad they split up the two Suffolk County semifinals this year. It used to be the best possible scouting opportunity. Two games, four playoff teams, one place, but two admissions as they always empty the stadium and refill it after each game. They say the reason is so the fans of the first game don't hog the best seats through both games. But I say it's the money from two separate gates. Naturally, the fans do a lot of grumbling over this.

We've got three juniors that are obvious D-1 prospects who will play a lot today. Kunkel, Ward, and Field. Four more obvious D-1 sophs in Rastivo, Spagnoli, Pall and LaMantia. They will get letters from coaches. Oh, will they get letters. Rastivo might wind up the number one goalie in his class in the country, which means offers from everywhere. But we are a senior team, and we will live or die today at Northport with the Class of 2006. Our defense will carry us to another unlikely road win against a very good team or we will be finished. I could be finished. We are an inch from falling out of the race and a yard away from winning it all.

On the bus ride to Northport I lay down a challenge to Westermann, who will again cover the All-American Dowd. Just exhaust the son-of-bitch, I say. Move your feet and stay in his way. I tell Westermann, if you do your job, we can't lose. If he beats you some, there are other ways we can win. But you can make that unnecessary. You can win this game by yourself. Show these Newsday people our defense is more than Sam and Matt. While I'm speaking Westermann looks like he has the weight of the world on his shoulders. Then I move down the aisle and tell Tsouris that he can win the game for us single-handedly with a dominant performance against their fabled midfield. No one thinks he can do it twice. Everyone thinks the first game was a fluke. Then I go find Droesch and tell Mike that . . . .

#

It felt like ninety degrees on the field today, and the game was played under modified heat rules, with mandatory water breaks every six minutes. Droesch scored first for us from the crease, on a dodge-and-dump feed from Tsouris. Dowd fought his way to the cage on a diving inside roll to tie the game just before the end of the first quarter. Chautin scored unassisted from the midfield to give Northport its only lead, but Kelaher quickly knotted the game at two on a dodge from the wing. Kelaher fed Beltrani as he cut to the cage to put us ahead again. Tsouris continued to dominate the faceoffs and he fed Kelaher for his second goal of the day. Tsouris scored again unassisted, but Northport responded. We broke for the half with us leading 5-3.

At the start of the third quarter we promptly handed back the lead. Luckey found the net for Northport while they were killing off a man-down situation. But Tsouris won another face-off and made it 6-4. Dowd fed Luckey for a man-up goal and the Tigers were right back in the game at 6-5. Burr swept hard right from the midfield and buried a low rocket to tie the score at six. Their crowd was into it. Our crowd was into it. The players were hot and thirsty, some of them cramping. Then came thirty-nine seconds that Ryan Kunkel will always remember and the Tigers would like to forget. Kunkel scored three goals in a blur, converting assists on the crease from Kelaher, Duggan and Tsouris to give the Patriots a 9-6 lead heading into the fourth quarter. The last of the Kunkel goals came with 1.5 seconds on the clock. The Tigers never recovered. Our poles held them scoreless in the fourth quarter as Dowd and Bartig went at Westermann and DeVore again and again and came up empty. With a tremendous physical effort we secured the semifinal win, number 699. As we got on the bus to leave Northport I think the Tigers in fact may be better than us, but we pure outworked them again. I could not be any prouder. That Tsouris was not named All-American is a travesty.

May 31

Still alive. What a feeling. What great kids we have. What role models for the next teams coming up. They never quit. They never back down. Davey MacCulloch, a former All-American at Hofstra, tells me his son Jake (8 or 9 years old at the time) looks up to DeVore and Westermann, his summer camp counselors. Little Jake came home one day and insisted his mother buy him boxer shorts, he was tossing his briefs away. Why, she wanted to know. Because Sam and Jake wear boxer shorts. So she gets him the boxer shorts and he starts wearing his jeans pulled low in the back, halfway down his butt . . . because that's how Sam and Jake do it. Here's hoping that they all pull up their pants real soon.

June 2

So it has come down to this: the Suffolk County final against West Islip will be played at Stony Brook this afternoon, weather permitting. We have been here before. We know what to expect. It rains most of the day, on and off, but not hard. Other parts of the Island are getting drenched. It's not bad on the North Shore, more muggy when we arrive at LaValle, and we warm up without incident and get going on time.

The first quarter is all Patriots, and we jump ahead like we haven't all year. It could have been even better. It should have been better. We had them on the ropes, but fell victim to side-arm, winding up and missing shots from ten-yards out instead of finishing the play from five. I wince at each miss, and know they will cost us. I just don't know how much. Droesch dodged from up top and fed Kunkel on the wing, who fired it low and put us ahead 1-0. The stadium erupted, but the Lions did not panic. Minutes later Tsouris forced a slide and fed Kelaher who made it 2-0. West Islip called time-out. I see Scotty calming his kids down. The stadium was rocking. Our bench was bouncing. This was the start we wanted. Tsouris keeps winning face-offs against Peter Mezzanotte, and when the Lions do get the ball, they are nervous, sloppy, and they throw it away or our defense repels them.

Kunkel scored again on a sweet feed from LaMantia to make it 3-0, still in the first quarter and the place goes nuts, our crowd smelling blood. Beltrani split-dodged and fired a wicked shot down low for a 4-0 lead and their Honorable Mention All-American goalie, Sal Barcia (Robert Morris), who never looks rattled, looked rattled.

Coach Craig is a great coach and he calms them down between periods and they come back angry at themselves and at us. The second quarter is even, scoreless, nasty and sloppy. But the pressure is building as time goes by. They need a goal bad. Another Droesch dodge from the midfield forced a slide, so Droesch flipped a nifty pass to Beltrani, a pass too high by an inch, forcing Alex to jump to make the catch and he hit the crossbar with his quick-stick as he returned to earth. You can see from his body language that Barcia can't believe his good luck or how badly his defense is playing. A five-goal deficit might have been insurmountable, even for the Lions.

At halftime we begged the guys to imagine the game was tied. We told them to expect a huge surge from the Lions. They were too good and too proud to go down easily. We know how tough these kids are. That this game was going to be a nail-biter. So what did we do? We went out and relaxed. A face-off went badly and West Islip broke down the middle and scored. Bang. DeVore had the bad luck to slip on the bottom bar of the back of the cage and dropped like he was shot. Bang, Justin Turri scores. A Ryan Kunkel goal on a Pat Nagle assist interrupted the Lion run, but we were reeling, and the game was soon tied at five.

Our first middies were tired and our second middies were physically and emotionally over-matched. We called time-outs to break the momentum, to get them rest and water, but we didn't save one for the end of the game, a fatal mistake. Tsouris, who played another magnificent game, carried our offense down the stretch, and scored an unassisted goal to give us the 6-5 lead with 3:30 left.

Almost immediately Mazzanotte responded with a bounce-shot from the outside, maybe one Steve-o should have stopped, but that's why you bounce them. Stuff happens. Bad hops, screens, deflections. Steve-o hands the ball to ref and gets ready for the next one. He has grown up so much in one year. With the game tied again and the crowd screaming Spagnoli runs to double Federico behind the cage when he maybe shouldn't have. Feds doesn't cough up the ball so Westermann is forced to slide to Spag's man. The crafty All-American knows a sophomore when he sees him, and immediately runs Spags through X, accelerates past goal-line-extended and gets his hands free for a second, forcing Tsouris to slide a yard, no more. Federico feeds Mazzanote up top for another bounce-shot through a screen, another smart play in the right spot, and the Lions score. We are down one and out of time-outs.

Still, in the final moments, an end-line double-team by Kresse and Westermann jarred the ball loose from Turri. They battled and the ball bounced around for a while until Westermann came up with it and headed up field. Time was running out on our clear so he hurled it long to Droesch, who was closely covered, but came up with the ball, anyway. Droesch turned and fed Duggan who fed the streaking Tsouris in perfect stride, and time slowed for me as I recognized all the earmarks of another play Ward Melville folks would talk about forever. Like Willy Passavia's goal, or Derrick Preuss's goal. To this day I can see those happen in slow-motion. The Tsouris bounce-shot slipped past the lunging Barcia, but missed just inches wide of the top left corner with twenty seconds left in the game. And our attack didn't back up the shot. They all stood on the crease, watching Nicky and hoping for a pass. This mental error means it is West Islip ball; and we have suffered a game-over, season-over, career-ending defeat.

Some of our players collapse to the turf like puppets with their strings cut. The players on the bench drop their heads and curse and tears well in their eyes. They have failed on the big stage they have always dreamed about. This one hurts in ways I can't begin to describe. I tell the guys to take it like men. We line up and shake hands and wish the Lions well, and the West Islip kids honestly and warmly express their appreciation for how far we pushed them, how hard we always play against them. Inside, I am devastated. I know in my heart I will never wear the green-and-gold again.

Back at the high school that afternoon I saw the saddest locker room I've ever seen. One after the other the boys hugged me and apologized for the loss and wept in my arms. I couldn't talk. My throat kept closing. In their minds some of them somehow thought that as long as they kept winning, I could stay at Ward Melville, that nothing would ever change. These last few weeks we were no longer playing for any round number of wins or a thirty-second Suffolk County title or even past Patriots—our usual motivators. They were playing to stop the clock for themselves and for me. And they failed.

Westermann told me later, when the game ended, he refused to fall down like so many of the Hofstra players had done the week before when UMass came back from the dead to beat them in the NCAA quarterfinal, all except for our guy Ryan Kelaher. Ryan held his head up, shook hands, put his stick on his shoulder and walked off like a soldier. Westermann saw Ryan a few days later and asked him why he did that. Ryan told him: "That's lacrosse."

When our clock read zero-zero, Westermann patted Federico on the gloves and walked off the turf with his stick over his shoulder. That's lacrosse, and life goes on. In 2006 Laxpower ranked us the 31st team in the country, with a 16-4 record (and 699 total wins.) Each of those four losses was by a single goal. West Islip advanced to play Nassau Class A winner Massapequa on Tuesday at Hofstra for the Long Island Championship.

It drives me crazy that we finished four goals from perfection, and a berth in the Long Island championship. I won't get over this for a while. We had a once-in-a-lifetime defense (3.75 goals against a game) this year, and it wasn't enough. We should have found a way to win it all.

June 3

We should be practicing.

June 4

Rain falls on Long Island as grim reality sinks in. Our underclassmen have New York State Empire Games team tryouts tomorrow. They are gone from me. I have lost them. Then it's Spring Sports Awards night tomorrow. Only six LI high school teams are still playing, and we are not one of them.

June 5

At our Spring Sports Awards we announce that Matt Kresse earned All-American honors and Sam DeVore received Honorable Mention All-American recognition. Matt routinely devoured his opponents with his strength and speed. His slides to the crease were powerful and he made some big plays on offense for us, too. Matt had a wonderful senior year after an outstanding junior year, and a summer season on the Gold Medal Empire Team. DeVore was selected to play in the Under Armour All-America game on June 18.

Earning All-County honors were Tsouris, Duggan, Kelaher and Westermann. Kunkel was named All-Division. Coach's Awards were given to seniors Droesch (Dedication), Nagle (Teamwork), Tsouris (Most Improved) and Westermann (Team Leadership). Our All-County players will participate in the Exceptional Seniors game later in the month. In my humble opinion, by the end of the season Nick Tsouris was the best midfielder on Long Island, and deserved to make All-American. We also told the team that if we had had ten guys named Mike Droesch on the field we would have never lost a game. Westermann and Nagle got the job done for us all year long. None of these four kids played a bad game all year. They were not our captains but they were senior non-coms, our sergeants on the front line.

After we handed out our individual awards I talked to the young guys about next year and to the seniors about college lacrosse, and how hard and fast a game it is, and how much fun it is, all at once, and how it lasts twice as long as their varsity careers at Melville. I pointed out that boys who did not get much playing-time at Melville could go on to star for their colleges if they worked. They have the tools. It has happened over and over again. Basically, I tried to cheer them up, and let them leave the program on a positive note. I told them when they finish with college they are automatically invited to play in the Alumni game.

None of them wanted to leave that classroom. We love this game and this team and this school. It was agony to say goodbye.

June 6

The three Long Island championship games are played at Hofstra. My guy Tom Rotanz and his Shoreham-Wading River boys hang tough for a half in the C Division, then get dusted by a terrific Cold Spring Harbor squad with boys going to Virginia, Penn, Duke, Dartmouth, you name it. In the Class A LI Final West Islip builds a 7-3 lead on Massapequa and then hands it back. The Lions finally win in two overtimes on a goal set up by Mezzanotte. That kid always comes through for them. I am an admirer. Tony Seaman at Towson is getting a big-time player.

In the nightcap Huntington destroys Garden City 19-10, and everybody enjoys watching Doc Daugherty get his comeuppance. Dean Gibbons, the boy who broke Matt Monfett's LI single season goal-scoring record, is shut out by Rob Shannon of Huntington, who is going to Lehigh to play for Ward Melville's Chris Wakeley. I see coaches with clipboards from Duke, Brown, Virginia, Princeton, Syracuse, Stony Brook, Army, Navy, Kean, Drew, Tufts, Trinity and just about everywhere else. Our boys should be playing in this fabulous recruiting showcase.

Between championship games I hear of a coaching vacancy at a smaller school in Suffolk County that doesn't compete with Ward Melville, and my heart begins to pound.

June 7

NY State Empire team tryouts are rained out.

June 8

The New York State semifinals are at Michie Stadium this year. West Islip is matched against John-Jay-Cross River. I don't think it will be too close a game. I think it just might be Scotty Craig's year. But we'll see. We should be playing in that wonderful stadium at West Point. It would have been a great learning experience for our kids. I play golf instead of making the trip up the Hudson.

#

That evening I hear that the Lions beat John Jay easily, 13-1.

So I was right. It was all about Long Island this year. And coach Mike Messere's West Genny Wildcats beat Orchard Park. They are coming to Stony Brook, and not to play us. What an atrocity. Stony Brook's AD Jim Fiore has told me he might need me to work the game from the press box. I might be the official timekeeper. How's that for irony?

June 10

West Islip beat West Genesee 7-6 for the title, after the Lions grabbed a 6-3 lead and then hung on for dear life. Neither team played well. We could have beaten them both with one more offensive weapon, or one good bounce. I think Mike Hoppey said it best at our Awards Night. "We were good this year, but not lucky."

The West Islip Lions were both and went 23-0 to be New York State Class A Champs. They beat us twice, by one.

In the B Division Championship game Huntington hammers Corning East 18-6, and Cold Spring Harbor wins the Cs over Christian Brothers Academy to complete the Long Island sweep.

June 13

I am a spectator at the US Open Golf practice round and can't get back in time for the All-County Dinner. But I am starting to feel detached from these post-season events, not needed, old and in the way. I hear that night I was given an award for a career of service to the sport. I wish I could trade the plaque in and keep serving.

I don't question the Three-Village school district's right to make a change, I only question the way it was done—and that it came with a dose of humiliation for me. I gave 38 years of service to the district as a teacher, department chairperson, and coach of different sports. I left over 370 sick days in the bank because I rarely took time off. Now I won't ever feel welcome on the sidelines of a big game. My green and gold clothes are obsolete. To be treated with such a lack of respect and appreciation was difficult for me to accept. To this day, no one has explained to me exactly what happened and who was responsible for making the change. I am disappointed in the way the situation was handled, that I would be shoved aside. But I will always root for the kids at Ward Melville as I move on with my life.

June 17

Regarding the national and state polls: If we're not first or second, I don't take much joy in arguing for a higher place. Tenth place? Who the hell cares? We didn't win it all.

The Ward Melville Alumni Game on Saturday is the first I have ever missed, because I am in Baltimore for the Under Armour Game. But I hear they had a fine old time, just like every year, and that Mike Hoppey served the role of host.

June 18

Six of our seniors play for the North Team in the Suffolk Exceptional Seniors Game at Stony Brook. Kelaher is the North's Offensive MVP. Duggan, Tsouris, Kresse, Westermann are all starters. They win easily 11-6 to complete their successful high school careers.

Later in the day down in Baltimore Craig Dowd scored five goals to lead my North squad to victory in the Under Armour Classic. What an incredible collection of talent in Baltimore, and what a pleasure to be associated with them. Being asked to be the head coach in the inaugural Under Armour All-American Classic was a wonderful honor. I was flattered that they thought enough of our program to extend the invitation. In addition to having the opportunity of working with the best lacrosse players in the United States, I was thrilled to work again with Jim Kaspar, Bob Macaluso, and Rick Mercurio. Jim and I coached the defense while Bob and Rick handled the offense. After coaching against these guys for so many years, it was great coaching with them. We worked well together and now I know why we had such a hard time whenever we played them—they are each great coaches.

Mercurio gave the North squad the pre-game pep-talk, and he made it geographical, put a New York chip on their shoulders: He said, "We lose this game and we're going to hear how great Maryland is at lacrosse for the next twelve months. "Those South kids out there," he said, "they think they're hot shit. And they think you guys don't really know how to play this game. They think the game already belongs to them."

Our guys were fired up and played hard and tough. DeVore de-sticked a guy, but the ball stayed in the pocket, so DeVore flipped the stick twenty feet in the air to shake the ball free. It kinda sent a message that we came to Towson to play rough. He also threw an amazing behind-the-back pass in traffic that started a fast break goal.

In response, the 6'6" 240-pound Will Yeatman (Notre Dame) crushed West Islip's Christian Scuderi (6'4" 200) along the sideline, a hit that people will talk about for years. Northport's Dowd got off to a bad start, trying to do too much. I watched for about five minutes, getting madder and madder, and then finally went to Macaluso. "Bob, if he doesn't knock that crap off I want you to yank him and tell him to calm down."

Bob nodded grimly. That's how Bob always nods. Maybe because he's a Vietnam vet, I don't know. Before we could say anything else to anybody Dowd scored the next two goals for us, and finished with five, winning the game's MVP Award. So timing is important. Have I mentioned that yet?

A North father from a non-hotbed state said after the game, "Our boys said they learned more lacrosse in two practices sessions with your staff than they learned in a full year at home."

One of the nicest moments for me was when Matt Ciamballa (Notre Dame) of Orchard Park, New York came up to me on the sideline—when it was clear we would win. He said, "Well, coach, there's number 700 for ya. I'm honored to have played for you."

What a great kid. What a great group of kids. What a great game.

June 20

As the farewell party approaches, and the door closes behind me at Ward Melville, I have the satisfaction that I did my best. Maybe not everybody appreciated it, and I'm sorry about that, but I came to play hard and win, and did exactly that. I never didn't play a boy because I didn't like him. I never played a boy just because I did. I always felt you put the best players out there that you had. You owed it to the others. This summer I still have the Four-Star Lacrosse Camp to help run in late June and then a trip to Italy planned with Lucretia. I will be busy and happy. Just not plotting and planning and scheming for next year. I miss it already.

June 21

It was nice to see people come to the barbeque at the high school to celebrate our program and what we have done over the years. Mick Foley and his father Jack Foley, our long-time Athletic Director. Bob Betcher, son of Bruce. Will Gray, our lifelong statistician. Melville Dads Anthony Casino and Gary Passavia came together, as always. A very funny skit mocking my mannerisms was put on by wise-guys Kelaher and Kresse, and was followed by some kind words from Mike Hoppey. My daughter and my grand kids were there, Lucretia, of course.

And the future of the program was there, too, sitting with their girlfriends. Next year's stars. Chris Day. Field. JC Ward. Rastivo, the second-ranked goalie in the country. Zach Pall. Matt Spagnoli. Cody Ferraro. Ryan Kunkel. Ryan Molloy. Greg Brennan. Josh LaMantia. Kyle Moeller. The boys' lacrosse program will go on winning. I can see that right in front of me. The guests gave me a gift certificate and the use of a condo in Myrtle Beach for a week. The school will hang a banner in the gym for me. But I don't want to go.

The sun was setting as I stood to make my farewell remarks. I kept them brief and thanked my friends and supporters. As I looked up from my notes each face I saw reminded me of other faces not there, and it all ached deep in my chest. I will miss everybody, these 1500 boys-grown-to-men that have passed through our program. I understand that. The good, the bad and the in-between. The honor of the association has been mine. I wish I had been better at this earlier. I have so many sharp regrets, and not about strategy or playing time. Just life as it roared by.

I look at Chris Day, a junior who has committed to play at Army, and I am so proud of him. What a place and what a tradition. I recall watching my own son play there his freshman year, a game early in the year, going on as the sun was sinking. And the game stopped dead, and the helmets came off, and all the players snapped to attention on the field as from far away they could hear the bugle as the colors were lowered. Day, who also plays quarterback and wrestles, will be a big part of replacing our departing defense next year. I can see in his eyes that he can't wait for his chance.

I do fine hiding my sorrow for a while saying goodbye to my players and their children and their parents, but I start choking up when Laurie DeVore hugs me and thanks me for making her son a man. I thank her for trusting me, because I was hard on Sam, and I demanded a lot. But if you don't demand things, you don't get them. Sam has given us a lot back. He now belongs to Petro and the Blue Jays of Johns Hopkins and if Sam thinks I was hard on him, he ain't seen nothing yet.

As the evening lengthens, one-by-one my people say farewell and drift away. Finally it is dark on the field, and even the catering staff (ex-players Nick Ward, Joe Higgins and Jared Blechman) working for my ex-player Stan Klesak are packed and gone. Lucretia and I are suddenly alone behind the school.

I look out at the dark stadium and imagine the houselights are on, the stands full and loud. There are so many things I could tell her about this place and those times, but not with a lump in my throat. After 46 years of teaching and 38 years of coaching, it was a constant struggle this year for me to be a part-timer, to let go. If it wasn't for the great kids I coached in 2006 and Lucretia's support and understanding, I don't know how I would have managed my grief.

I notice the stars have come out over Guam as we walk to the parking lot. Ours is the only car left on that vast patch of concrete; and I remember that I was usually the last to leave.

The End

Epilogue

In October of 2006 I got another job that helped ease the pain. I was hired as the full-time head lacrosse coach at Mt. Sinai High School, a smaller public school five miles down the road from Ward Melville. The athletic director who took a chance on me was Scott Reh, a lacrosse All-American himself at Rocky Point. My first assistant coach was Harold Drumm, an All-American defenseman at Ward Melville who played at the University of Massachusetts. Our junior varsity coach was Jay Negus, also of Ward Melville and UMass fame. The team colors are black-and red, not green-and-gold, so I had to mothball much of my wardrobe. No longer a Patriot, I am now a Mustang.

The kids and the community opened their arms to me and we had a big publicity event with my 700th win in the first game of the regular season. It was great for the program and much appreciated by me. Just for winning one game, we were on the Madison Square Garden channel, in Newsday, in Sports Illustrated. Suddenly nobody was asking: what's a Mt Sinai?

There were emotional adjustments to make and I made them. I won't kid you. It wasn't easy. But Ward Melville moved on and now so had I. The boys who played for me at Ward Melville during 2005 and 2006 have gone on in college to be extremely successful. DeVore won an NCAA National Championship, Duggan and Mazzone a MAAC championship. Droesch, Molloy and Ben-Eliyahu each won NESCAC championships, Kresse won an America East Conference title and Westermann an Ivy League Championship. Tsouris was an immediate starter at Yale. Droesch was a two-time captain at Tufts. Mazzone was a three-time captain at Siena, DeVore a captain at Johns Hopkins, Redko a captain at Ursinus, Westermann a captain at Brown . . . and they are not done yet.

Meanwhile, at Mt. Sinai high school we got busy with the little kid program some smart dads had started previously. We got into the off-season workouts, running, winter leagues, position clinics, changing the culture of Mustang lacrosse. Frankly, lacrosse was not the marquee sport at Mt. Sinai. Football was, and might still be. When I arrived, the seniors on the lacrosse team actually took a party trip out-of state during the middle of their season. Big tradition, I was told. And a really bad one, I replied. No wonder they've never won anything. We needed to make lacrosse incredibly important to them, to grow their dedication to the game.

I give credit to the kids. They bought into it quickly. Then, by exposing them to difficult preseason games and scrimmages, we gave them the confidence that they could play with the big-name schools. That was good for their self-esteem, and it carried over into their play. We made the playoffs in 2007, but got knocked out early by a well-prepared Babylon team.

The following year, our second season, we added Rick Mercurio from Sachem East to the Mustang coaching staff and built our varsity around one of the Island's best defensive units. (That sounds so familiar.) Here I'll give one last piece of advice to young coaches: Go out and find the best possible staff. Bring in your own Harold Drumm and your own Rick Mercurio. They were such a blessing at Mt. Sinai, that I didn't have to teach everything myself. I had the same thing at Ward Melville with Bill Martens, Bruce Betcher, Ray Weeks and Herb Friedman in the program. We had great lacrosse coaches everywhere you turned. The head coach makes the big decisions, and then turns the staff loose to do their thing. I was always lucky to be able to do that.

Happily, the 2008 Mt Sinai team got better as the year went along. They battled their way out of Suffolk and then got "off the Island" with a surprising upset of highly ranked Cold Spring Harbor at Hofstra. Subsequent wins over the Hudson Valley champion and in the state championship game against Corning East gave Mt. Sinai a Class C title, the school's first, in only the program's seventh year of existence. Our senior goalie Andrew Zoly was phenomenal down the stretch. Big-time recruits Mike Chapman (UPenn,) Mike Sweeney (Yale), James O'Brien (Adelphi), Shane Henry (Cornell) and Connor Fitzgerald (Delaware) played nightly to their fullest capacities. Unsung guys like Eric Baslov (Springfield) played like seasoned All-Americans.

For me, it felt wonderful to return to the middle of that field and watch a new group of boys celebrate the best moment of their lives. It felt wonderful to win one with Lucretia in the stands, that she could observe the hubbub and help pick out the championship rings. It was nice to prove to the lacrosse world that I hadn't lost my touch.

In 2009 the Mustangs repeated as Suffolk County Champions and then lost 10-6 in the Class C Long Island Championship game to the eventual New York State champion and third-ranked team in the country, Manhasset. So now they are really excited about lacrosse in Mt. Sinai, and the younger boys want to follow in the footsteps, and that dumb senior trip is a thing of the past. Driving to school these days I see little boys walking on North Country Road, cradling the ball in their lacrosse sticks, wearing Mustang lax gear. And so it goes.

Edwards Brothers,Inc!
Thorofare, NJ 08086
22 March, 2011
BA2011081